SUGAR, GRAVY, PLEASURE

SUGAR, GRAVY, PLEASURE

An Indie Odyssey in Peterborough

PETE ELDERKIN

Copyright © 2024 Pete Elderkin

The moral right of the author has been asserted.

Apart from any fair dealing for the purposes of research or private study, or criticism or review, as permitted under the Copyright, Designs and Patents Act 1988, this publication may only be reproduced, stored or transmitted, in any form or by any means, with the prior permission in writing of the publishers, or in the case of reprographic reproduction in accordance with the terms of licences issued by the Copyright Licensing Agency. Enquiries concerning reproduction outside those terms should be sent to the publishers.

Troubador Publishing Ltd
Unit E2 Airfield Business Park
Harrison Road, Market Harborough
Leicestershire LE16 7UL
Tel: 0116 279 2299
Email: books@troubador.co.uk
Web: www.troubador.co.uk

ISBN 978 1 80514 428 1

British Library Cataloguing in Publication Data.
A catalogue record for this book is available from the British Library.

Printed and bound by CPI Group (UK) Ltd, Croydon, CR0 4YY
Typeset in 11pt Minion Pro by Troubador Publishing Ltd, Leicester, UK

CONTENTS

Acknowledgements ix
Preface xi

The Beginning 1
Background 4
The Laughing Gravy 13
The Pleasureheads 22
The Sugar Club – The Warm-up 35
1991 – Fifth Avenue Kick-off 40
1992 – Special Delivery 53
1993 – Britpop 60
1994 – It Ain't Gonna Happen 64
1995 – Mis-Shapes 71
1996 – Fenland Bermuda Triangle 78
1997 – Don't Lose the Ticket 86
1998 – TFI Friday 90
1999 – The Metropolis Lounge 95
2000 – Sound of Silence 102

2001 – Tension	109
2002 – The People, the People, the People	114
Epilogue	120
Final Thoughts	124
Love and Thanks for All the Inspiration	125

ACKNOWLEDGEMENTS

Copyright reserved contributions from Steve Jason, Kevin Robinson, Martin Rowe, Mary Leen Hagger, Matt, Mel, Louise Hartje, Richard Grange, Kirsty Mulhern, Leo Lyons, *ESP Magazine*, The Destructors/Lee Mason and Tony Judge.

Mis-Shapes
Words and music by Nick Banks, Candida Doyle, Mark Webber, Jarvis Cocker and Steve Mackey.
Copyright © 1995 Universal/Island Music Ltd., BMG Rights Management(UK)Limited and Steve Mackey Publishing Limited
All Rights For Universal/Island Music Ltd. administered by Universal-Songs of Polygram International Inc.
All rights for BMG Rights Management (UK) Limited administered by BMG Rights Management (US) LLC.
All rights for Steve Mackey Publishing Limited administered by Songs of Kobalt Music Publishing
All rights reserved. Used by permission.
Reprinted by permission of Hal Leonard LLC.

Release the Bats
Words and music by Nicholas Edward Cave and Michael John Harvey.
Copyright © 1982 BMG Rights Management (UK) Limited and Mute Song Limited.
All rights for BMG Rights Management (UK) Limited administered by BMG Rights Management (US) LLC.
All rights reserved. Used by permission.
Reprinted by permission of Hal Leonard LLC.

PREFACE

Just to be clear, this story about eleven years in Peterborough is not about being incarcerated for an arduous prison stretch at His Majesty's Prison in East Anglia. It's about a newly acquired freedom of musical expression and an electrifying stretch of social history. This is an unapologetic celebration of working-class culture and the amazing, fun times that were created together by everyone involved. It's a celebration of a great period in alternative music history and the effect it had on a small, but beautifully formed, band of outsiders in a culturally starved provincial city. The culture was truly special and should, in some small way, be recognised and appreciated. I wanted to let the story be known and it deserves to get a mention. So, in a time that could never be repeated, here's the story of the Sugar Club from 1991 to 2002.

Our city isn't associated with musical success nor is it a place that regularly features on the tour dates of any up-and-coming groups. For a long time, it was a cultural desert and we had to make our own entertainment. It was the largest city area without a university or polytechnic in the UK, which gave us no regular exposure to great live music or the chance to see our idols in action. This was the backdrop to growing up in the area. We wanted a place to go to that celebrated the music we loved.

I live in New Zealand now, some 20,000 miles away, and the distance makes me think about and really appreciate what a truly special time and place it was. I miss the warmth and '*aroha*' (love) of my home city. I may take the mickey out of Peterborough at times, but I feel I'm well qualified to do so and it comes from a loving place.

I first had the idea to write a memoir about the club way back in 2019 and it has taken five years to pull it together. This coincided with me giving up alcohol which gave me the necessary drive and time needed to do it. I don't want to get too preachy, so I won't go into all the benefits of that decision. Even so, I still found it hard to sit down and get on with the book. I had made a start and written a lot, but then I felt it was the people at the club who made it special and that to make the book work, it needed contributions from them and their unique viewpoints. Once I decided to ask for contributions, it gave me the impetus to finish the book – it would've been embarrassing to be the one who stalled the project. Midway through the process, we had a beautiful baby, so it was a challenge to balance work and home life with another delivery – the book.

All the stories in the book happened to the best of my memory and they are obviously my take on events. Some may see it differently and I guess when their own book comes out, they can tell it from their perspective. People may feel the book is a bit childish or ego-driven, but there is no point in going to all this effort and then watering it down to make it more palatable for others – better not to bother in that case. You must be true to your own sense of humour and the way you think is best to proceed.

Hopefully, readers will find it interesting. The locality doesn't matter to pick up on the importance of relationships and how they worked together or didn't. I suspect there won't be a plethora of similar books about music in our city, but it's great to reflect on what was important locally and keep that social history alive. I'm sure I've forgotten people or stories that I should have included, so please forgive me.

When you look at memoirs, they are often from successful people who come from families with plenty of privilege and I feel that I'm often more interested and drawn to working-class stories. I loved the autobiographies from Frank Skinner, Bobby Gillespie and John Cooper Clarke because they were honest, interesting and I could relate to parts of them, despite coming from totally different parts of the UK.

The working title of this book was *Eleven Years in Woodston*, which was my local suburb. However, my friends implored me and insisted that I see the bigger picture – to become broader and less parochial with my writing. So, after a lot of persuading, I reluctantly agreed to change it to *Eleven Years in Peterborough* and eventually to *An Indie Odyssey in Peterborough*.

Special thanks to Martin Rowe, Mary Leen Hagger, Kev Robinson and Steve Jason for their contributions to the book. It was great to get their input. Thanks to our other contributors, too, who have all added their own perspectives, namely Matt, Mel, Louise Hartje, Kirsty Mulhern and Richard Grange. Thanks to Leo Lyons for his band photography and Steve Rolls. Thanks to Tony Judge for the expert advice and perspective on the design. Thanks to Jane for her love and support along the way.

THE BEGINNING

'Feel for You' by Chaka Khan slowly faded out with the last twenty seconds of music. The dance floor was full. Young, happy people on a warm, late summer's night. All evening, the music had been light, fun chart hits and there were smiling faces everywhere. There were a few seconds of silence and then the stylus hit the groove of the next record, followed by a short pause and some static, before a deafening, shocking sound started up.

> Whoah bite! Whoah bite!
> Release the bats, release the bats!
> Don't tell me that it doesn't hurt
> A hundred fluttering in your skirt
> Oh don't tell me that it doesn't hurt
> My baby is alright
> She doesn't mind a bit of dirt
> She says 'Horror vampire bat bite'

As the dance floor suddenly cleared, five black-clad boys in skinny jeans moved in and started dancing wildly. Two minutes and thirty-one seconds of scary, raw, full-on, sensory-overloaded alternative rock fury ended with a silence, open jaws and staring eyes. As it finished, I quickly grabbed the twelve-inch record back from the stunned DJ, slipped it into the inner white sleeve and walked away. As we left, there were a hundred sets of eyes on us. The atmosphere in the place was now decidedly frosty and let's just say that the locals weren't looking happy. Our walk turned into a sprint almost straightaway as we ran towards the exit doors. I looked back and saw four skinheads put their pints down, jump up, throw on their light-green flight jackets and start following us. Oh no. I could hear my heart begin to bounce through my chest and into my ears, and then the cold air hit us as we reached the outside of the venue. A quick glance back confirmed my worst fears, as the four men were now running after us. I could hear their Doc Martens hitting the floor.

We sprinted across the tarmac of the car park and Stu fumbled with his keys to his car. *My goodness, we're going to get absolutely battered*, I thought. I glanced around and all my friends looked terrified. Stu's hands were shaking, but eventually he managed to open the door and we were inside. We locked the car doors and the engine started just as the men arrived. They tried to pull open the door handles and bang on the window. Then, one of them jumped on the back wheel hub and lay across the back window, banging onto it and shouting at us, just centimetres away from where we were sitting. The biggest guy landed on the front bonnet, calling us 'chickens' and telling us to get out of the car. We sure as hell didn't want to be anywhere but inside the car. My hands were shaking and I was feeling sick. He said they just wanted to talk to us, but I had a sneaky suspicion he might be lying – just call it intuition.

The other two guys repeatedly kicked the car bodywork as they burned off their frustration. They couldn't quite get to us inside to give us a real beating. We didn't say a word back to them and tried to avoid eye contact, staring at our feet. Stu finally drove off sharply with the two skinheads still holding onto the car. He couldn't see much as we moved through the dark, empty car park towards the street lights. They were trying to break the glass now and punch their way into the car in a final effort to get to us, but the motion had them beaten. As we sped up, they decided to jump off and roll away.

We screeched out of the car park and drove through the town, only stopping when we reached the local police station for safety. There was a light on in the station and we pulled up and parked near the door, sitting in the car silently. I could hear my heartbeat pulsing in my head. As the minutes passed, we started to calm down and feel less scared – a very close call indeed.

That was one of our nights out – not a usual one, but not a totally unusual one either. My friends and I occasionally visited that disco in a local town and it had been packed that night. We'd had a fun time until the abrupt end. The mistake that we made was to ask the DJ to play some music for us. It's fair to say that 'Release the Bats' by The Birthday Party was polarising music where we come from. Sat in the back of the car, I briefly thought, *Wouldn't it be great to have a club where we could enjoy our own music without the fear of getting beaten up?*

BACKGROUND

In 2019, my home city of Peterborough was awarded the accolade of 'Worst Place to Live in England'. I was surprised when I read this story online and thought it unlikely to be true. It was a survey in the *Daily Mail* asking for nominations and the votes were then compiled and announced. I was convinced that it was all a big misunderstanding. It would be corrected in the following year's survey and an apology issued – perhaps it was all just an admin error. To be awarded the title once might suggest the possibility it was all a giant mistake and a fluke result. In 2020, though, the city not only topped the chart again, but this year it was a bit different. This year the voting was not just for eligible places in England, but for the whole of the United Kingdom as well. So, even with all those extra other added countries in to choose from – namely the whole of Scotland, Wales and Northern Ireland – we still managed to top the poll for 'Worst Place to Live in the UK'.

This second award confirmed many people's feelings about the city. Those two awards partly inspired me to write about my own times in Peterborough – to set the record straight (there are actually some great places there and some different scenes), but also, to be honest, I wrote out of badness, I suppose. I love my home city and I wouldn't have the same resilience I have coming from anywhere else. I have a pride in our place, despite some media-bashing, and it has made that pride grow stronger. If people still don't like it, then that's fine. Don't go there and don't live there. As they say on the football terraces, 'No one likes us; we don't care'.

I grew up in the Woodston area on the south side of the River Nene and I loved it. It was a down-to-earth area and we had a lot of people who worked in our local factories, like Redring and Hotpoint, which made household whiteware. We had a lot of new families come to the region as I grew up, moving to our city from London, encouraged by Roy Kinnear's TV campaign to attract people out of the capital. There was quite a wide range of kids from different social backgrounds at our school. I loved playing football with my school friends, mainly Italian mates, playing large games at St Augustine's school field. There was a large Italian community in the area and I would often be the only lad playing of English descent.

My parents moved to brand-new housing in the 1960s, from Ramsey in the countryside. I was the youngest of three children and I suppose they stopped having any more when they found one that they liked. My older siblings may disagree, though. In truth, that theory doesn't hold water when looking at our family photo albums. There are approximately two hundred photos of my brother, then about a hundred of my sister and two photos of me – one taken on my third birthday and one on my seventh birthday. We lived near the London Brickyard chimneys and during my schooldays, we would often venture across the railway lines onto their site to mess about in the dangerous brick kilns that made the red bricks. I always loved watching Fred Dibnah, a TV steeplejack (google it), because he would often be on top of those great structures several hundred meters high. As I grew up, the chimneys were all toppled one by one over the course of several years. It was great fun to watch the two-hundred-meter brick structures flop to the ground with a mountain of dust enveloping everyone.

My dad worked at Bennie Lifts and made passenger lifts for tower blocks and my mum had various jobs supporting the family.

I'd sometimes go to see our team, The Posh (Peterborough United), with my dad in the Glebe Road stand at the football ground. Our team mascot was a gentleman in morning suit with tails, a top hat, a walking cane and a monocle. For those uninitiated to the area, this could be a bit misleading, as that outfit wasn't really very common on the local streets. At the start of these visits, I'd be at the front of the stand with a wooden stool that he'd made, so I could see over the wall onto the pitch. It was often a raucous crowd with lots of banter from the crowd around us directed at the opposing team. Our area of the ground had a lot of men from all the local companies, mainly the physical manufacturing industry. The crowd passed the time in matches shouting out banter to put off the opposition players. They might remind them that they were a bit chubby or else that they had long, girly hair – anything to get a reaction. As I got older, my poor mum also had to take me to see The Posh for a couple of full seasons in the Fourth Division. Football was a big part of my life as a kid and that has never left me.

I went to the local comprehensive secondary school, which was a bit like *The Inbetweeners* TV show at times. A backdrop to much of that time, though, was that if there was anybody that was too different, they would be open to teasing or bullying. It was a feature of school life and standing out too much could mean that your school sports gear might be thrown into the showers, possibly followed closely by you.

I also developed a bit of a cutting wit myself, which was a defence mechanism, I guess. For a short period at school,

I was lucky enough to get my very own bully from the year above, who looked a little like Billy Bunter, but minus the cheerful demeaner and smart blazer. I remember one time I bumped into him as I left the newsagents; it was about 7am on a Sunday morning and I was about to start my newspaper delivery round on my bike. He'd been insisting for some time that he was a top-ranking karate black belt and now he decided he wanted to demonstrate his kicking skills. At school, it hadn't been too hard to avoid him, but out of school it was much harder to get away. He promised faithfully that he would stop his demonstration kick before any impact on my head. I was quite gullible at the time.

For those not acquainted to it, the Peterborian accent is possibly a bit hard on the ears, although obviously you don't realise that as a child. I remember we had an older teacher from Liverpool, Mr Clarke, who once pointed out our 'funny' accent to our entire class. I was surprised to know that I had an accent at all, as we all spoke the same. He demonstrated this by asking the class how we pronounced 'computer'. Everyone knows that it is phonetically pronounced: 'com-puu-arr'. 'Beautiful view' was the next example and that is pronounced 'boot-a-full vuu', so we really had no idea what he was banging on about. We just knew that *he* had a Scouse accent himself, but we weren't sure if it was a deflection or a projection technique as we didn't have a psychology option in our school. There was no way of knowing which one it was, as we didn't know if he knew that *he* had the unusual accent, without mentioning his own funny accent, which may have got us a belt.

My own musical journey probably started with exploring my sister's records. She was into 2 Tone records like Madness, The Specials and Fun Boy Three, and was also mad about The Beatles and The Jam. The Jam were regularly played at home and I loved their sound and the meaningful lyrics, which really connected. I didn't feel that same connection with some bands like Genesis and Pink Floyd, other than liking the odd track.

I got into my own music via *Smash Hits* music magazine and eventually bands like Adam and the Ants, and New Romantic music like Thompson Twins or Duran Duran, who were in the charts at the time. Then came The Cure, Big Country, Echo & The Bunnymen and bands like OMD (Orchestral Manoeuvres in the Dark). These were all major label bands, not indie (independent label) bands, but they were slightly different from the normal, similar pop bands on the face of it. I then moved onto discovering Joy Division (via a mate's older brother), New Order, Cocteau Twins (who we saw while at school), Bauhaus and Talking Heads among others.

That was my music discovery journey from the teenage stage onwards, but before that is the growing-up stage that no one ever mentions. It's inevitable that you'll discover music that you like initially but doesn't last the test of time. We didn't have many records in my parents' collection, so there weren't many options. I would really enjoy the *Paint Your Wagon* cowboy film soundtrack, which had songs like 'There's A Coach Comin' In' or the moody deep voice of Lee Marvin on 'Wand'rin' Star'. We had the *Fiddler on the Roof* musical record and we liked 'If I Were a Rich Man'. There was also the seven-inch of *Summer Holiday* by Cliff Richard and The Shadows, and we imagined being on the red double-decker London bus travelling to Greece in the lovely sunshine just like the film. Generally, we went on holiday to Hunstanton or Heacham for a week, but we had vision.

I started to discover different genres and loved The Sisters of Mercy who played at the local technical college – the first real gig that I'd seen. The support band that night were The Destructors, who were a local punk band that played under a different name as they were banned in the city. The Sisters opened up a world of gothic music, just as it was starting to grow in popularity, and then I worked backwards to discover bands like Siouxsie and the Banshees and The Clash, and then alternative influences much further back like Iggy Pop and Velvet Underground from the 1960s. I loved Orange Juice, Aztec Camera and Lloyd Cole and the Commotions, and by then I really started to know the indie scene via weekly music papers. I loved R.E.M. from around the time of the *Reckoning* album, which had the breakthrough single 'South Central Rain', though the whole album was great. The Smiths then came out and hit the mark, and just blew everyone else away. Their 'Hatful of Hollow' compilation of BBC Radio sessions had all the best tracks on it, with awesome, meaningful lyrics, too – they moved music forward to the next level. They captured the moment, the look and the time so perfectly and with a sense of humour. Fans of those bands had to be content with an occasional appearance on *Top of the Pops*. There was no mass market for them or saturation radio play, just the odd top-forty single, perhaps.

The Glasshouse at the Key Theatre, promoted by Ann Johnson, would provide local, regular Sunday lunchtime performances in the city by popular national bands and local bands. These daytime gigs enabled us to see real musicians up close as we didn't get many decent bands playing regularly. We would go and watch the likes of John Otway, Billy Bragg, Doctor and the Medics and ranting poets/comedians like Porky Pig and Attila the Stockbroker. Attila was great and took the time to talk to an awkward teenager. He even encouraged me to write some (awful) poems, which he kindly included in his fanzine. I also enjoyed The Gaslight club, a relaxed Sunday night venue held at a Catholic club. It hosted some bands and a lot of great comedians like Jo Brand and Jack Dee. I remember seeing Ted Hawkins play at the venue, who did the *Songs from Venice Beach* album, which was a privilege. Visiting this place was a ritual for a couple of years; it was a nice place to end the weekend and get inspired for the week to come.

After school, I was minus A levels, but very few students in our school went on to get a degree from university and that wasn't ever on my radar anyway. The universities of Cambridge, that cultural mecca, were just forty miles away, but it may as well have been a thousand miles. 'Going to Cambridge' was a phrase mainly used by our football hooligans about to run amok whenever the two teams met in Division Four.

I was young and immature when I joined the workforce and got a job at the passport office. It gave me an introduction to real-life working and it's fair to say that I initially spent a lot of time messing about with my friends there. I was sometimes in the call centre, where concerned customers would ring to find out when their passport was going to arrive. We would sometimes take a call and add a colleague, pretending we had a crossed telephone line with three people on the call. My workmate and I would then instigate a mock argument using a heavy Fenland accent and he would insist that he was first on the call and that the other person (the real customer) would just have to wait his turn. I should add that we always did solve their problem, but only after much mucking about first.

The office also taught me about cultural institutions such as Secret Santa. Whereas most staff received minor gifts, my friends and I would often gift wrap unusual items to make it more fun. We literally wrapped a car engine part one Christmas and three of us carried it carefully into the office early on the morning of the present opening. It wasn't really a gift that a middle-aged lady expected to receive and she indeed looked very pleased with the size of the present until it had been unwrapped. It must have been tricky to get it home on the bus. Another less than subtle game we had, after tea breaks, was to walk past the office of a particularly annoying manager and simply throw the dregs from our coffee mugs – if he wasn't in there, of course. I recall he had to get a new carpet fitted after a couple of years.

We had multiple strikes during my years at the passport office, due to management reducing conditions in line with government pressure. These were interesting times when colleague was pitched against colleague. During strikes, there would be a picket line of us striking staff all day, standing outside of the office building to stop the mail from physically arriving. Management knew the Post Office workers would not cross an official picket line, though, but one morning we caught mail going in via a dodgy contractor van trying to beat the strike. There was a verbal altercation between several pickets outside and this staff member, who was gloating about how much overtime he'd be making (striking staff did not get paid). This was a very interesting political time and I became the branch secretary for the PCSA (Public and Commercial Services Union), fulfilling a desire to push back on the Margaret Thatcher-era policies. However, work for me was always the number two priority in my life behind my interest in indie/alternative music. A great bonus of work was that I had access to a large, fast colour photocopier that I could use for printing flyers for my social events.

I was usually skint within a few days of my monthly payday and that's despite not paying any board to my mum and dad. The wages helped to pay for nights out and new records. We occasionally had work social events, which involved drinking copious amounts of lager/beer, and they were fun, exciting nights out. They had an annual pop quiz event with cheap booze on offer, which ensured it was a chaotic night of in-jokes and loud laughter. Banter and high spirits were so boisterous that in the end the event was abandoned, as the compère couldn't be heard over the hubbub. The recriminations flowed the next day at work and staff complained to the boss about our behaviour. He was an old-school type in his fifties with a beard and glasses, who had moved up from London as a 'high-flying' civil servant with no connection to the area. My friends and I were called into the office and he decided to ban us from the social club for a year, without much discourse on the matter. We thought it was a bit of an overkill but had the last laugh as our work friends then boycotted the social club.

As I got older and started drinking with my friends, there was a general social mistrust of anyone that looked or felt 'different' in the bars. It could be a rough city at times, and you needed to keep your wits about you if you were out socialising. Walking around the city centre and looking 'unusual', like alternative music fans did, could literally get someone abused with a chance of a punch in the mouth. This unease was particularly felt by many of society's 'tribes' like punks, post-punks, new romantics, goths and alternative music fans, and anyone looking 'weird' would have to be aware of their surroundings.

Living near the bottom of our close, by the Celta Road bus stop, were some skinheads (of the dangerous racist variety), who were in their early twenties. On the way home after a night out, I got verbally abused and chased on the way home as I went past their house. After that, every time I returned home after a night in the city, I would sprint past where they lived. I knew once I reached the bottom of my close that I'd be safe.

My best friend was hospitalised once, which was very traumatic. I wasn't out on that night, but several lads chased him and beat him up in the Bretton shopping centre. His crime was simply having backcombed, black 'gothic' hair and a long trench coat. This had a direct impact on all of us and made us even more aware of the need to be safe. I wanted to create a safe space in the city for all those waifs and strays that didn't adhere to the social norms of the time and looked different. A place for people who loved the alternative music and lifestyle, which just wasn't the norm at the time.

THE LAUGHING GRAVY

I started my first club night at The Crown pub on Lincoln Road, Peterborough, which was a couple of miles out from the city centre. I named it the 'Laughing Gravy' ('LG') after the small, white terrier dog in the Laurel and Hardy films. The DJ playlist came from current independent music that me and my friends loved, plus classic tracks from the seventies and eighties.

I started the club with a few friends from school, so we could hear 'our' stuff. Pete was tall and dark-haired, with a long, dark floppy fringe and a short back and sides. Dean was the king goth with dark, backcombed hair and an occasional bit of cheek make-up. Andy also DJ'd and he looked like a young Christopher Plummer, but with a floppy fringe. We had other guest DJs, too. We'd also take our favourite records from our parents' collections, the lads bringing the likes of The Beatles, The Monkees, 'Son of a Preacher Man' by Dusty Springfield or 'These Boots Are Made for Walkin'' by Nancy Sinatra. *Fiddler on the Roof* never made the cut then, but the 'Rock Around the Clock' single by Chubby Checker did get an outing. We also loved some great music by Australian bands we were getting into, like The Birthday Party, Hoodoo Gurus, Lime Spiders and The Triffids, who we discovered on the John Peel radio show.

Here's a flavour of the LG playlist from that time: Abba, Aztec Camera, BAD, Bauhaus, Beach Boys, The Beloved, The Bible, Billy Bragg, My Bloody Valentine, The B-52s, Bob Dylan, Bob Marley, Buzzcocks, Camper Van Beethoven, The Charlatans, The Clash, Cocteau Twins, The Cramps, Creedence Clearwater Revival, The Cult, The Cure, The Danse Society, Dave Pike Set, Deacon Blue, Depeche Mode, Dexys Midnight Runners, Echo & The Bunnymen, ELO, Elvis Costello, Faith No More, The Fall, Felt, The Go-Betweens, Hoodoo Gurus, The House of Love, The Housemartins, Hüsker Dü, Iggy Pop, The Jam, James, James Taylor Quartet, The Jesus and Mary Chain, John Lennon, Sid Presley Experience, Johnny Cash, Jonathan Richman and the Modern Lovers, Joy Division, The June Brides, Killing Joke, Kingmaker, The Kinks, The Kingsmen, The La's, Levellers, The Lemonheads, The Loft, Lloyd Cole, Lou Johnston, Lou Reed, Madness, Manic Street Preachers, The Mock Turtles, Morrissey, New Model Army, New Order, Nick Cave and the Bad Seeds, Norman Greenbaum, Oasis, OMC, Orange Juice, Paul Simon, Paul Weller, Pearl Jam, Pixies, The Pogues, Pop Will Eat Itself, Prefab Sprout, Primal Scream, Prince, The Proclaimers, The Psychedelic Furs, Public Image Ltd, The Redskins, R.E.M., Ride, Robert Wyatt, Sinéad O'Connor, Siouxsie and the Banshees, The Sisters of Mercy, The Smiths, Spear of Destiny, The Specials, The Spencer Davis Group, Stealers Wheel, The Stone Roses, The Stooges, The Stranglers, The Sugarcubes, The Sundays, Talking Heads, Teenage Fanclub, Tennessee Ernie Ford, That Petrol Emotion, The The, Tom Petty, Tom Waits, T. Rex, The Triffids, U2, The Undertones, Van Morrison, The Wedding Present, The Who, The Wolfhounds, The Wonder Stuff, The Woodentops, World Party, Yazoo and many more.

Initially, we would get around a hundred people turn up every night – friends aged between sixteen and twenty mainly – and it just got busier and busier as time went on. It was awesome to play our favourite music and we also began to learn how to DJ. Often, we'd be let down by scratched records that skipped, bringing the music to a sudden halt, or we had dodgy styluses, so I do feel bad for our early audiences. Sometimes we'd simply not have the next record queued up and ready to go in time as the last song finished. When that happened, there'd be an awkward silence as the whole room looked over to the DJ booth, wondering what had gone wrong, and you'd sheepishly put on a song ten seconds too late. It's fair to say that we learnt as we went, with our fair share of mistakes.

Diane was the publican; a short-haired woman from North Yorkshire who had eyes in the back of her head. She liked our enthusiasm, but got annoyed with the shenanigans of our young clubgoers. She caught anyone who was very drunk and throwing up outside, as well as any couples getting amorous in the ladies' cubicles.

I also started promoting a couple of live acts at The Crown to go alongside the vinyl music we played on the turntables, which were part of the provided gear. One of the first live acts I booked was a comedian from the Midlands called Ted Chippington, who told surreal jokes in a deadpan style. His show went down a storm in Peterborough and he, improbably, went on to have a minor hit with a cover of The Beatles' 'She Loves You'. It was the first of many gigs at The Crown and our own band, The Pleasureheads, would occasionally play, too. The LG started to get a loyal local following. I ran the place every few months for a couple of years, but it was miles from the city centre so it wasn't ideal if attendees wanted to end up drinking in the city later in the night. The capacity was becoming too small for the two hundred or so that came, even though there was no real capacity monitoring.

I found a bigger venue and managed to move the club to the local Irish club, The Shamrock, on Brook Street in the city centre. The entrance was on the right of the front of the building, up a set of steep stairs. Downstairs was a members' club frequented mainly by a rough-and-ready mix of hard-drinking men, with plenty of builders and tradies. We were based upstairs, so were separate from the main drinking club. The room was a large rectangular space used for weddings or functions with a dusty old carpet, the original colour of which was not clear. The relationship worked brilliantly and there was a mutual respect among the two different groups of outcasts. They left us alone to do whatever we wanted and locals were too wary of the Irish guys downstairs to risk trying to disrupt our music club upstairs. Even the local police steered clear and didn't check us for underage drinkers, thankfully, although we were directly adding to the numbers of young drunks in the area every weekend.

We cohabited in the club very happily for several years and we built a loyal following of music lovers and 'alternative' types. Mick Creedon was the owner – a diminutive, suit-wearing chain-smoker, who took me under his wing by being very supportive and even built me a stage for bands to play on. Once I got the one-foot-high wooden stage installed, I could start to run my indie/alternative club and book national bands, which gained us even more interest and the numbers took off straightaway. Brendon was our barman and occasional bouncer, who once single-handedly removed three drunken, fighting lads from the main club – so upstairs was a walk in the park for him. We had a dedicated security guy; it could get feisty when drunks would sometimes try to burst into the club. The advantage of a steep narrow staircase meant they could be seen wobbling upwards and then be dispatched relatively easily back down again.

The Laughing Gravy quickly became a haven for alternative music fans, punks, goths, industrial fans and any other independent music styles. You would hear music that wouldn't be played anywhere else, even in the most popular UK bars or on commercial radio stations. We attracted waifs and strays and almost immediately had a great vibe. There was always humour and fun. You could dress as you wished at our club and nobody would bat an eyelid. Nightclub dress codes were very strict and common at the time, so we were very different to the norm. Getting into a standard city-centre nightclub meant dressing like every other punter in the city, with trousers not jeans and dresses for women – and that just wasn't our thing. Our crowd were a real mix, but often comprised dark-coloured clothes and fans of goth or post-punk. It was a place separate from all the mainstream pubs and nightclubs in the city. We were also 'gay-friendly' before the term was invented, as there was a general low-level homophobic attitude in the UK at the time. Anyone was welcome at our club; people just needed to like the music and the attitude.

Before long, The Shamrock became so popular that most weeks, we had a queue down the steep stairs and onto the street outside. By this time, we also had some indie promoter envy happening. Every man and his dog wanted a piece of the 'indie action' and were trying to set up gigs or clubs. One night, when a promoter also happened to have a rival event on elsewhere in the city, we had a bomb scare. The likelihood of our venue being on an IRA hitlist was very low, given that the main drinking club was frequented exclusively by the Irish community. Apparently, a bomb threat had been phoned in by a young bloke and two local policemen, and their dog, were duly dispatched to the club, looking a bit bored. First, they turned off our music and then evacuated (or shooed out, more accurately) everyone from the club to the pavement outside. They wandered around for a few minutes as everyone waited, then they came down and said it was 'all clear'. I'm pretty sure the dog wasn't trained in detecting explosives, but possibly the canine had had some kind of professional development course and knew there were no explosives present. Anyway, within five minutes, everyone was back inside the club, laughing and partying like there was no tomorrow, relieved to still be alive and celebrating our lucky escape! Time for some Pearl Jam.

I put on numerous groups over the next several years, including Levellers, New Fast Automatic Daffodils (also known as New FADS), Carter the Unstoppable Sex Machine (Carter USM), The Wood Children, Teenage Fanclub, The Mock Turtles and Ride, all of whom were high in the UK independent music charts at the time. The Levellers' gig was very interesting as they had a following that literally took over the venue and the local streets around the venue. They turned out to be lovely people and crew, but I must admit that as a young promoter, I was intimidated by their appearance and the travelling buses, raggle-taggle followers and the dogs they brought with them. The gig was packed to the rafters, with sweat dripping off the roof. I believe we also had a short power cut to contend with that night, but it was a good-natured, fun crowd. All these gigs were amazing and the shows coincided with big indie singles like 'Sheriff Fatman' by Carter USM and 'Big' by New FADS.

As our popularity grew, I again needed to find an even bigger venue. I started to expand my horizons and think bigger by starting a monthly night, 'The Big LG'. I held these at the Peterborough United Football Club bar (The Posh Club), which had a capacity of around five hundred. It tied together football and music, and it was a venue that no one had tried to use before. On its opening night, I really wasn't sure what would happen as the room looked massive when we arrived and I was concerned that very few would turn up. I'd hired two 'proper' door staff (nice guys, too) in case of issues, who wore black suits and ties. They gave me some comfort that there'd be no security issues. The club manager was an older guy from

Sunderland who'd seen it all and seemed encouraging and supportive. Over the next few hours, a massive crowd turned up and playing in this bigger venue was so awesome. I'd hired a much better sound and light system to match, so it was very 'beefy' (that's a technical term). The gig went down a storm. As it was a local gig for me, I'd decided to have a few pints and walk home, rather than drive to the venue. At the end of the night, I was sat down, smiling, quite drunk and oblivious among a pile of drink glasses. The only thing I hadn't reckoned on in my planning was an issue with pint glasses. For some reason, the crowd struggled with glass pint glasses and when they were moshing and dancing like crazy, the glasses got smashed – a lot of them on purpose by a few destructive lads, I think. At The Shamrock, we'd had plastic glasses and there hadn't ever been an issue. The amiable manager was very unhappy about all the breakages but was compensated by the hundreds of pounds he made from the bar takings that night. He said I could continue, but suggested I needed to move to 'either plastic glasses or possibly baby beakers'.

The crowd had been large, a lot more than I'd expected, and it showed that with the right occasion, there was a big crew interested in our style of event. Capacity wasn't really a concern at the time, as the health and safety laws seemed loose, and we frequently had five hundred to six hundred or so people in the place, I'd guess. The timing for the expansion in venue size was brilliant as many of the bands that we loved were now starting to hit the mainstream like The Smiths, James and The Stone Roses and while we didn't know it at the time, the popularity of our music was set to grow and grow. I kept the gigs as monthly ones at most, so that it held an appeal rather than just being the weekly norm.

It was fun playing The Big LG gigs at The Posh Club and we even played at a one-off night at the massive city-centre nightclub in the city, Shanghai Sam's nightclub, which had a capacity of a thousand plus.

And in all the time that the Laughing Gravy club was taking off, I was also in a local band called The Pleasureheads.

Matt

My school in the eighties was a tough place for someone with alternative music tastes. The popular kids were all listening to Five Star and 'Rock Me Amadeus' and I would have the piss taken out of me relentlessly for listening to The Smiths and The Cure. Hovering around the legal drinking age, the cool kids were all trying their luck at getting into Shanghai Sam's nightclub with varying degrees of success, but this really held no interest to me and my new friend, Adam – he had moved to our school because his previous one had no sixth form – who shared my own musical tastes.

We heard a rumour that there was a place that played our kind of music and had the occasional live band. Our plan was hatched and the next Friday came round soon enough. Donning newly purchased Stone Roses T-shirts from Our Price, we got the bus into town and made our way to The Shamrock Club, climbed the stairs and paid our £2 to get in. It was like entering a whole new world. I had finally found my people. The playlist was everything I'd hoped for and more – The Wedding Present, The Wonder Stuff, The Stones Roses and Happy Mondays, to name but a few. It was the first time I'd heard 'Roadhouse Blues' and I remember making my way up and asking the DJ who it was. The next day, I purchased *The Best of The Doors* from Andy's Records.

Over the next few weeks, I spent all my money from Saturday jobs on Doc Martens, band T-shirts, entry to the LG and Newcastle Brown Ale. It was well over thirty years ago, but feels like yesterday.

Kevin Robinson

My induction to the Peterborough indie music scene was on Thursday 8th February 1990. I was studying for my A levels – tapes and copies of *NME* would always be strewn around the sixth-form common room. A mate suggested we go and see Ride, who had just released their first EP – the one with the red roses on the sleeve. This would be the first of many occasions that we'd climb the rickety staircase to The Shamrock Club. Being underage, I immediately felt intimidated by everyone with long hair, smoking and drinking cheap cider or Newcastle Brown Ale. To get to the toilet meant navigating your way through empty bottles on the floor and stepping over numerous couples copping off together. My memory of Ride is of a row of long fringes, intense strobing and squalling feedback. It was dead exciting.

I remember seeing so many bands there. At one gig, the lead singer managed to punch his head through the actual low ceiling. The dance floor was disturbingly bouncy and often, during a particularly aggressive mosh to 'Kennedy', we wouldn't have been surprised to find ourselves falling through the floor and landing in the laps of the hostile drinkers in the pub below. Nights would usually end by trying not to fall down the stairs, avoiding all the snakebite and black that had been vomited up on the curb outside, before heading home via the obligatory stop at the Chilli Hut.

THE PLEASUREHEADS

We heard John Peel's distinctive voice coming through the radio speakers, "The first coming up from The Pleasureheads. They are variously Joe Maccoll (drums) and Andy Colton (bass). Andy Donovan. Sorry, Dave Colton (bass), Andy Donovan (guitar), Kevin Murphy (guitar), Pete Elderkin on vocals and percussion, and Dean Nichols on vocals and percussion. From Peterborough, I think…"

Having grown up listening to late-night radio, the dream was the chance to record a session of songs for the BBC Radio 1 John Peel show – a man that we idolised. He'd helped launch and promote recording greats like David Bowie, T. Rex, The Clash, The Smiths and hundreds more. My friend, Dean, and I desperately wanted to be in a similar group. We'd been friends since we got into trouble for cutting each other's hair at primary school. There was only one issue: we couldn't play anything musical. A minor issue we thought and decided that drums would probably be the easiest thing for us to learn. Really, it's just whacking things and if it was in time, then that would be a bonus. In the end, we alternated on drums and vocals, making up for our lack of ability with our enthusiasm and passion. We were going to be the singers and front men on stage for a rock group and luckily we found some talented guitar players. We had Andy from the LG on rhythm guitar and our 'bass monster' was Pete, who first introduced us to Manchester bands like The Smiths and Fad Gadget. Mark was on jangly lead guitar – he was fun and into some of the 'C86' bands like Primal Scream, The Primitives and Shop Assistants.

The new band was run in parallel with the fledgling club nights for a while, but it took over the weekends more frequently. Being in a band fed my musical appetite and learning to play live and entertain a crowd helped me to understand how to promote a stimulating, fun, entertaining event. Talking and banter with the audience in between songs was part of our live band experience and it helped me with DJ'ing at the LG events and talking with the crowd. Without the band, I don't believe the club side of what I was doing would've developed at all.

After a year or two of practising and several chaotic early gigs, we managed to get a record released. This was realised with the help of a local schoolteacher and supporter, Andrew Clifton, who kindly paid for the single. It was a very proud day for us all to get 'Falling Man' and 'Don't Fake It' released as a seven-inch vinyl single. We folded all the white sleeves and put them in their clear plastic pockets. It was a long-held dream come true for all of us.

We recorded it in Guildford at the University of Surrey, where a friend, Jim Abbis, was studying and he engineered it for us as a mate. He went on to work in the music industry, producing the likes of Arctic Monkeys and Adele. We didn't have much of a promotional plan other than to play a few gigs and do the usual 'rites-of-passage, rock band-type things'. I just gravitated to the role of chasing radio play and reviews for us. We did get played a fair bit on local radio, courtesy of fans writing in to implore the DJs to play our track. In truth, though, many of those fans had curiously similar writing to mine (apart from the ones written left-handed). Eventually, I ran out of names and aliases, so the requests dried up.

Our big breakthrough happened after a long, exciting wait after sending out the records to all the national music papers, including *NME*, *Melody Maker* and *Sounds*. The single was reviewed first in *NME*. It said, 'Falling Man motors along with strumming guitars and a beat more usually found in the tastier songs of the Lemon Droppies. The Pleasure Heads have taken the attractiveness of being a wimp band and meshed it into a harder rock format. The result is a streamlined, aggressive sound reminiscent of The Bunnymen before they discovered the power of the echo.' Amazingly, it received the coveted 'single of the week' for the whole of the UK. To say we were chuffed and overwhelmed would be a big understatement. We also had a review in *Smash Hits* by the legendary Mark E. Smith from The Fall, who said our single '…was an amazing sound… at least it's got some f***ing balls about it for a change!'.

We first met the legendary DJ John Peel at a gig in Bedford, at a Wedding Present/Soup Dragons' gig, and we gave him the obligatory cassette tape of our music (note to reader: if you can't find him on Wikipedia now, he's probably been cancelled from music history). There's no doubting his influence on popular culture at the time was immense and he started the careers of dozens of great British rock artists. Fortunately, he liked the tape and invited us onto his Sunday evening radio show on BBC Radio Cambridgeshire. We'd just released the first single 'Falling Man' and he wanted us in for a chat and to have the track played on his radio show. On our drive into Cambridge, we were listening to the car radio and Peel mentioned that he was feeling hungry and that he fancied some onion bhajis. We decided to stop off at a local Indian takeaway on the way in and took the hot dish into the studio with us, which he loved. As he was eating the food live on air and talking, he was so happy that after he'd played the single once, he took it off the turntable and played the other side of the record for us. He was great fun; we loved meeting him and even better that we made him content with Indian food.

We practised twice a week in the back room of the Swiss Cottage pub. We had Kev join the band on lead guitar. Usually, Andy or Kev would start with a guitar riff and the rest of us would join in and jam together until a song would hopefully appear. Dean and I looked after the lyrics for the songs that we did the vocals on. When we started playing live, our main aim was to musically get through the actual songs without making mistakes and, over time, we got better and better. Getting gigs was hard, though, as no venue wanted to take a chance on an unknown band, and to become a known band, you'd have to have done some gigs, so it was a bit of a catch-22. Over time, however, we built up a local following, starting with friends watching us and then slowly building up an audience.

I would generally ring and write to venues for gigs and hassle promoters, but what I could get wasn't always ideal. I would sometimes have to take a gig where we had no guarantee of any cash – not even enough to cover petrol costs. We just tried to play in front of a few new people whether it was a few miles or forty miles away. Some gigs could be quite daunting, too. One time we had a gig at a tough, heavy rock bar in Huntingdon, with a hostile crowd. When using the urinal toilets before the show, a couple of drunken locals made a threat to batter us if it wasn't a good show. This sort of pressure was scary and not likely to relax anyone into producing a great show. There were no security staff at the gig and the threatening blokes, who were bigger than us, were on the floor level with us, drunk and only half a meter from our faces. The pub was called The Lord Protector, but even Jesus would think twice about intervening in a fight at that place.

The gigs were dark, smoky and seriously loud. Our rhythm and lead guitarists would both try to be heard the most in the sound that we created and this led to louder and louder gigs as we had no one to arbitrate on what the mix should be like. We would always utilise the whole stage (if we had one) and always gave a hundred per cent in no uncertain terms, so people were never bored. Dean would, at most gigs, throw himself off the stage and directly into the standing audience during a song and sing into the microphone for the rest of the song from the floor. We worked hard and had some great gigs around the country, and some crazy nights out. Over the next couple of years, we got a few positive reviews in the national music papers. Jonathon Romney wrote: 'Plenty noise, plenty sweat, plenty contortions shook the stage… These men have a nice healthy glow to their cheeks and a massacre in their heads… with extended extracts from the Tommy Cooper joke book'.

Our shows were getting bigger and pulling more people in to see and support us. We tried to be entertaining at our gigs, but also serious about the actual music. Playing live, we would stop between songs and talk and joke with the audience, Dean and I would talk and try to spark up some banter with the audience. We would do gags and occasionally audience participation jokes. In one of his regular gags, he'd ask, "What's pink and wrinkly and hangs out your underpants?" If someone in the audience shouted out, "Your grandmother!" he'd say, "No, it's your penis, mate!", but if someone shouted out the answer, "Your penis!", he'd say, "Oh, that's terribly rude. It's your grandmother, of course!" Childish, but we felt it was funny at the time. We'd always plan to have something worthwhile to say at a couple of points in the gig and I tried to take that into DJ'ing by preparing at least something relevant or funny to say to try to connect at the club. When the gigs were great, the crowd were engaged and happy, then the buzz from that would last for the whole week and nothing could touch it.

We played a Sunday lunchtime hometown gig once and as we were hungry, we decided that we'd break the taboo of not eating while on stage. Office workers could eat their sandwiches at their desk, so why couldn't bands eat, too? Anyway, that was our rationale at the time. So, just as we were about to go on stage, we placed a pizza order and timed the two big pizzas to arrive just as we were mid-performance. At the show, we had about three hundred people sitting on the floor, spread out. Then, in between songs, the pizza delivery guy duly turned up, wearing his motorbike helmet and hi-vis vest, and waded through the audience. He had to make his way through the crowd, hand us the hot food and then collect his cash. It was then we realised that we didn't have enough cash and we had to ask for coins from the crowd to help pay the delivery man. We then handed out some pizza slices to the crowd as the poor delivery guy slowly made his way back out, stepping past the seated audience. I think we realised after that episode, which went on for a while – too long, really – why bands don't eat on stage. Could you imagine rockstars like U2 trying the same gag at one of their gigs? Bono taking a big bite into a hot roast beef and gravy sandwich at the start of the song, just before the vocals start on 'Pride (In the Name of Love)'? It'd be funny and puncture some rock images, though.

Peel's interest in us helped to get us noticed and we signed for the second record release. After that great start, we were able to secure a recording contract with Ediesta Records, part of Red Rhino Records, who were based up in York. The next release was 'Holding On' and Kev was lead guitar on his first record. He was an enigmatic, frantic live guitarist, an exponent of the slide guitar and a fan of Blues players like Robert Johnson. He cut a mean, serious figure with slicked-back hair and a long-sleeve shirt and waistcoat. The twelve-inch record had the iconic photo of Harold Lloyd, the silent movie star, hanging desperately from a clock face on a New York skyscraper building – a literal reference to the song title. We managed to get some good reviews again and interest was certainly on the rise.

The next release was a twelve-inch featuring 'Treasure', 'Madonna Eyes' and 'Something You're Above', which did well and had several BBC Radio 1 plays and generally good reviews. The *NME* single of the week review said: 'Sometimes... a walk through grunge valley where monstrous guitar riffs and stuttering drumrolls leer down at you from every angle. The Pleasure Heads say 'Up your bum Maggie' and we spit in delight'. It's probably the best, most accessible track that we did and it sounded good on the radio, too.

Following that, we had an album out called 'Hard to Swallow', which got okay reviews – seven out of ten in *NME* – but it didn't exactly set the world on fire. Arguably, it didn't really capture the live sound. We managed to get a recording contract with Black Records next, part of FM Revolver, and we were record labelmates with The Stone Roses (a band we loved) and Crazyhead. The guy in charge was Paul Birch, who'd fallen out with The Stone Roses and they'd thrown paint around his office. The Pleasureheads' next release was a Black Records Barfly EP twelve-inch ('Within Reach', 'There's No Change' and 'She Said') in 1990. 'There's No Change' had my lyrics/vocals and the song was about the violent people and attitude that existed towards alternative music fans and others during that period.

This EP had Dave Colton join us on bass guitar and Joe Maccoll took over on the drums. Dean and I focused on vocals and congas in the six-piece alternative rock group. Dave and Joe had been in seminal Peterborough punk bands, Destructors and Destructors V, which I loved, so actually being in a band with them was a privilege and great fun. We benefitted from their experience as a competent rhythm section and their ability to play music in time. Joe was Scottish and had dark, short hair, and played drums with his shirt off. The vocalists started to use his conga drums (not to be confused with bongos, which are much smaller) at the front of the stage, which added more percussion to our sound and they looked good, too. Dave was a jovial chap and relaxing company, with short, light hair and he could play any rock song because he had been playing in bands for years. We had a lot of banter with him, which sometimes centered on his frugality in getting in rounds of drinks. I'd never known anyone 'forget his wallet' as often as him or be the last to the bar to order.

We played an early show with Then Jericho in our hometown, which was a Sunday afternoon open-air show with a couple of thousand people present in the sunshine. Our mate, Rob, a daytime local radio DJ, was compèring the show. The headliners seemed on the verge of pop stardom and were a bit sensitive. He made them even more sensitive and teased them by reading out the start of their setlist to the crowd. Their security man tried to grab the setlist off him on stage and he had the microphone turned off, so the crowd couldn't hear him. So, let's just say he could be provocative from time to time, but we loved him and his style, pricking the bubble of these prima donna wannabes. He'd known us for a while and he had great music knowledge. We'd met him in The Still pub, which was a haven for an alternative, mixed-aged crowd for years and was the scene of many drunken nights out for Peterborians. He loved to tell stories and I loved listening to his tales, which invariably revolved around bars and rock music. He came onboard as our manager and helped get some order into our gigs and live sound, but he was no shrinking violet.

We all had so many laughs and bonding experiences travelling together on the road, driving to gigs around the country. The gigs were raucous affairs at times and we had quite a few adventures while playing. In Coventry, after one show, we were threatened by three imposing doormen who said that they'd keep our gear if we didn't cough up a contribution to the cost of the event. There was a stand-off as these rather large Brummie numpties physically stood in the way, stopping us from leaving with our band equipment. Luckily, our Scottish drummer, Joe, who could be quite stroppy himself, called their bluff and just brushed past them and straight out to the van with a hi-hat stand. They were shocked and stepped back, thinking he must be either mad or very tough. We all quickly followed suit, grabbed the gear and got out of there as soon as possible. At a separate gig, we faced an irate fan who wasn't happy with our performance and demanded her train fare back home. Tough crowd, but we don't give refunds. All the trips were fun, though, travelling around the country and spending many late nights in a cold van, driving back to Peterborough with the lads and with music gear packed to the gills. I'd often be sat in the front with Rob having some drinks and chatting and laughing all the way home back up, or down, the A1.

We had a local gig once at The Tropicana nightclub with Balaam and the Angel, the popular Scottish goth group. They were an established band who'd been on the scene a long while. We were excited to be playing with them and we had celebratory bottles of champagne (well, cheap fizzy wine) on stage with us while we played our support slot. Then, at the end of our set with our home crowd, which had gone down well, we opened the bottles and sprayed them about like we'd won a grand prix. Balaam were very grumpy as they reckoned we'd sprayed 'champagne' into their sound monitors. They grabbed Dean by the throat and threatened to kill him as we all tried to pull him away from them, resulting in this unsightly tug of war on the side of the stage, with them pulling him one way and us pulling him the other as they were calling us 'bastard support bands'! Not a great look in front of the audience, but I guess it's a bit rock and roll.

We played support gigs with Jesus Jones at The Junction in Cambridge, which went down well until the end when I mentioned Posh had beaten their football team recently. We played a couple of gigs in Hull with The Housemartins (including Norman Cook, aka Fatboy Slim, on bass guitar). We didn't particularly connect with them as they were a bit older and we didn't have much in common, but you could tell that they were on the way to bigger things. That was the show when we first ate on stage, simply because we grabbed some takeaway after the soundcheck because we were hungry. The support group only had a very short set, so they finished quickly and we decided to take the kebabs onto the stage with us and eat between songs. I promoted a show with the brilliant The Godfathers at The Tropicana, and we played support for the gig. By me promoting shows, we were always able to be the support band on the night too, which was cool, and sometimes even provide the music between bands. For that gig, I remember I needed my mum to help me with the food rider, as I was struggling to get the cheese and tomato sandwiches ready on time.

Apart from the usual petty local band rivalries, we had a generally friendly vibe with local groups. Around those years, there were lots of groups playing, including Boysdream, Dave Reid, Kiosk 2, The Detours, Jilted Brides and others. We played a couple of local gigs with local punk group The Frantix and liked them. The shows were good, although Andy Frantic, their guitar/vocalist, did threaten to kill both singers, on separate occasions, as he didn't appreciate our cheeky banter.

Unfortunately, we did argue and bicker among ourselves from time to time at rehearsals and sometimes when deciding who'd have to drive to and from the gigs. One of our most bitter battles was about who would drive to a gig in the snow a couple of hours away. All the lads liked to have a drink, so no one wanted to be the driver. Sometimes we'd draw lots to decide, apart from

Dean who didn't drive, but when it was someone's turn and they didn't drive, it could turn into a massive fight among the band. One fight occurred when we drove to a gig in Rugby in heavy snow and forced our way two hours along the roads in awful weather. Before we'd even gone on stage, we were having a shoving match at the venue, still arguing about the driving situation. A guy watching us said it was worth coming to the gig just to see what was going to happen next and it was better than *Eastenders* for drama. The funny thing was that although we'd got safely to the venue, the locals didn't even turn up to the gig due to the terrible weather conditions, so after all that effort and arguing, we ended up playing a show to about nine people.

We had another hometown gig upstairs at the trendy Viva la Rock club, near the River Nene in Peterborough. At that show, Dave played a support set for us with just vocals and guitar, and on the gig posters we gave him and a washing machine equal billing, just for a joke. At the 'climax' of the concert, we smashed up this gutted washing machine we had taken on stage with us (à la *Einstürzende Neubauten*). We then picked up that washing machine and, with the audience in tow, carried it outside, then walked the two hundred metres to the city-centre bridge and ceremoniously threw it over and down from the middle point, splashing into the river below. I should add here that this was pre-recycling days. Anyway, that Hotpoint 9534 model washing machine is probably still spinning cycles in the water down there. Much later, when we were joking about the gig, we reminded Dave about his equal status to an inanimate object. He retorted that at least he had not been blown off stage by the washing machine, unlike us. Touché.

A year later, we were invited to record a John Peel BBC radio session by his producer, John Walters, who rang me at my mum's house to tell me one sunny afternoon. It was a surreal moment to get the phone call and achieve a long-held dream with The

Pleasureheads. The 'session' of four songs was recorded at the famous BBC Maida Vale studios in London one weekend, with Dale Griffin from the seventies rock band Mott the Hoople as our producer. The songs were then played on the radio spread across one two-hour show. And so it was that on the 25th of May 1989, the band all gathered at Donny's house and listened to BBC Radio 1. Just like that, we had finally achieved the dream we'd had for many years. It was an amazing feeling to have finally got into the company of so many amazing bands before us (and we all felt unworthy). In retrospect, it was a purple patch for music around those years and either side of our John Peel BBC radio session being broadcast in 1989 were Dinosaur Jr and The Wedding Present – great musical company to keep. Peel had also selected Nirvana and the Pixies for sessions that year, which showed how amazing rock music was around that period. In the end, it may only have been the hot onion bhajis that made Peel continue to support us, but we'll never know.

A while after those releases, I was invited out for my midweek birthday with Dean. We were having a fun night in The Cherry Tree pub, talking about music and the fun events that'd been happening. He gave me a present, a twelve-inch record by Billy Bragg called 'Sexuality', which is a fantastic pop tune with amazing lyrics. As we got to last orders, we were talking about my upcoming short overseas holiday to Greece, which was happening the next day. Dean said that the band had discussed it and they wanted to carry on with the weekly band practice while I was away, and that they wanted to carry on without me. I wasn't quite sure what to say. At that moment we had to leave the bar as they were closing the pub and then, before I knew it, we were outside. I was hit by the cold, frosty air and soon I was off on my bike to cycle back home in the dark. I felt like throwing away my awesome new record, which was balanced in its new HMV plastic bag on my handlebars, but I didn't want to lose it and there was nobody around to see the grand gesture anyway. So that was that and it was never discussed again. I decided then to eventually close the Laughing Gravy, forget the band and for my sole focus to be on starting my own alternative club.

THE SUGAR CLUB – THE WARM-UP

As the Laughing Gravy nights grew bigger and we built up a large, loyal group of friends and clubgoers, it was time to look for a different venue. Some local promoters were setting up rival nights and even hiring the same venue, which lacked a bit of imagination on their part. We sometimes heard of less positive experiences at our venue and people assuming it was an LG event.

Around that time, I got a phone call from Steve Jason, a popular local DJ and concert entrepreneur, who ran a live concert ticketing service. He was a face around town and most people knew him and his distinctive blond highlights. He came from a legacy of club DJs at the time who, for whatever reason, had two first names as their DJ stage name. We arranged to meet and chat at Miss Pairs café bar in the sunshine. It was our local version of a Parisian sidewalk café, but instead of the premium paid for a street-view table in Paris, it was cheaper on the outside seats at Miss Pairs as you were regularly interrupted by people asking you for spare change. Steve suggested a partnership to combine his promotional and event skills and my 'indie/alternative' experience with the LG.

I wanted a culture where clubgoers who were into alternative music had a safe, fun place with a lively atmosphere to go to. You could be into indie, ska punk, goth or whatever the hell you wanted. You could dress as you wanted and nobody would bat an eyelid. I decided to name the venue the Sugar Club after The British Sugar factory in Woodston. It was the place that turned sugar beet plants into processed sugar; during my childhood, it made the whole city smell of sugar beet for months at a time and we grew to like it. The band even seriously considered a scratch-and-sniff sticker of the fragrance on one of our records. I used to visit their workers' club with Andy to play snooker and we'd get drunk on two or three dry ciders.

The Sugar Club started on Saturday 16th August 1991 as a weekly club with the intention to build on the success of the Laughing Gravy nights. I would DJ and coordinate the other DJs. Steve suggested we use the Fifth Avenue nightclub, but a part of the nightclub that wasn't currently used in the evenings. It was a three-hundred capacity at any one time, I think, using a 'one-in, one-out' system running from 9pm to 2am.

Working with Steve was good as he looked after all the promotions stuff and he was an ideas man. He was always thinking of new offers for admission prices, fun flyers or other ways to keep it exciting. He also looked after the sound and the speakers and lighting, while I looked after the music, turntables and CD players we used. He'd hand out flyers just before we opened to make sure anyone going out drinking in the city would know we were open and what time to get there. I was able to focus on the music and figure out what new music to play, and who we needed to have DJ'ing and when, to keep it fresh.

In the early days at Fifth Avenue, we sometimes had some commercial club types wander into our club by mistake. To get the right people in the club to achieve the right attitude and atmosphere, we had to be selective. For us, if someone was 'overdressed' or 'too smart', then they weren't in the right place. We didn't want the stereotypical clubber dressed for the big nightclubs in our place and they would be incredulous when we turned them away from the door – it was awesome. We also had late after-pub drinking hours, so people would try to get in – some of whom had been ejected from another club in the city centre – and cause trouble. To combat this, as with all UK nightclubs, we had the 'expertise' of local doormen to keep order. The doormen for our club were the same ones from the main commercial nightclub, as we were in the same building but hired our area separately. In the early weeks, there were a couple of occasions when the doormen had to eject groups of lads who really were in the wrong club and just weren't nice people. It took a fair bit for the security to remove these guys and it could be at the extreme end of violence. One guy was throwing punches at the doormen, before he was ejected via the emergency-exit stairs. Eventually, with a doorman holding each limb, he was literally thrown out through the fire-exit door head first onto the hard concrete paving of Laxton Square – and it was raining. Ouch.

Some of the first doormen we had weren't comfortable managing punks, goths and indie kids. Eventually though, after a few weeks, we found a sympathetic couple of doormen who were more open-minded to our clientele. They built a good rapport with our clubgoers and were happy to 'work our doors'. One of those great doormen, Steve, was a black, lean guy in his thirties who was trained in martial arts and had a soft spot for our club. He was smart and had various ways to find out if attendees were old enough to attend. The required age was eighteen and in those days many kids had fake driving licences or borrowed ID from an older sibling. He would ask the young-looking kids their horoscope sign. Often, they would look bemused and be unsure of the horoscope sign as they'd pinched the ID from their older sibling – he caught out quite a few that way. On other occasions, he'd make the lads do twenty press-ups in front of the long, waiting queue before they could enter the club. It was all done in fun and jest, and he always ended up letting these muscle-challenged, red-faced kids in the club in the end. Yes, it was totally embarrassing for them and that's just the way it was – nobody wrote to the local paper and social media wasn't around to post a video about it all. It also meant that anyone who persevered in the long queue really wanted to be there and therefore we really wanted them inside, too.

Steve Jason

I'd been running coaches to concerts across the UK since 1982, taking people to see bands like The Smiths, The Wonder Stuff, U2, Simple Minds, New Order, Echo & The Bunnymen, The Stone Roses and Happy Mondays. I opened the box office in the old arcade in 1990, selling tickets to anything and everything, so I knew there was a fair demand to see alternative bands in the area. I'd promoted shows with alternative bands recommended by Mick & Sarah Jane (remember them?), who presented an alternative show on Hereward Radio in the evenings, but I'd never actually done a club night, as such. However, in early 1991, I struck a deal with Howard Cooper, the manager at Fifth Avenue, to rent the upstairs room, known as the VIP Suite. At the time, Howard was concentrating on trying to get the main part of the venue to turn some numbers as it was struggling, so to have a promoter offer him £300 for basically opening a spare room up was 'easy money'.

The initial idea was to run two nights aimed at the older clubbers in the area who'd had enough of the regular clubs, but it was tough to get the over twenty-fives out two nights on the bounce. Kev Robinson, who worked in the box office on Saturdays, would keep on at me saying that there was a demand for a 'proper' alternative club in the city, but I wasn't sure. The Attic, which had recently opened, had tried to start such a night, but had quickly had to bring more dance music into the mix to make numbers work. At the same time, Pete was – without doubt – the main man on the 'alternative gig scene'. He'd had a great run of shows at The Shamrock Club and some good club nights under the Laughing Gravy banner, but he'd been hindered by the midnight licences of the clubs he'd used. Jon McManus had also, I think, been running 'Danceteria' club nights at the PSL club in Lincoln Road, but again he was hindered by the midnight licence.

So, I asked Howard if he'd be up for an 'alternative night' in the VIP Suite on a Saturday. The non-negotiable was that there would be no dress code – bear in mind that, at the time, Fifth Avenue and the rest of the nightclubs in the city all had a 'no jeans, no T-shirt' policy. He didn't mind; he just wanted a bar take with minimum hassle! So, I reached out to Pete to see if he was interested. I think by that point Pete had realised that he was struggling to take his nights at The Shamrock any further with the midnight licence and he was losing out to The Attic – a later licence can sometimes be a bigger attraction than the music being played (sadly). He'd look after the music and I'd take care of the promo and the front door. We had a deal.

With Kev and Nathan hooked in as DJs alongside Pete, we were ready to roll. I'd already installed a sound system in the room with the decks nicely positioned on a grand piano, so the next step was all about getting the word out (in pre-internet, pre-social media days). We were lucky, of course, because we had the box office to use as a flyer point – anybody coming in to book tickets for anything alternative was handed a flyer for this 'new' night starting soon.

1991 – FIFTH AVENUE KICK-OFF

In August 1991, we started the club. I had Kev Robinson and Nathan Ciriello as the other DJs with me. I'd split up the evening into thirty-minute segments and decide who was playing when, and they'd arrange their own music to play during their sets. Earlier in the evening, we'd usually showcase some of the week's new releases and play a lot of requests for the crew that arrived soon after the doors opened. We always had a diverse mix of alternative rock, older classic sixties rock (but not heavy metal), indie, but not too much dance music initially (other than some pop classics like Abba or Tom Jones). We generally filled up pretty quickly and would usually be full within an hour, then it stayed that way all night. I was chuffed that the start couldn't have gone any better and we had a lovely feeling in the club.

The club became an instant hit really and we immediately had a large queue forming around Laxton Square before we opened and throughout the night. Our grand opening was perfectly timed with the 'grunge' influx of music from America, which was totally by chance. The most famous and best of the genre were Nirvana, who blew apart the crap, pop music that was around the charts at the time. There was some great new grunge music coming though, including Pearl Jam, Mudhoney, Dinosaur Jr and others on Sub Pop record label. It was a definite influence on the general music we played and the great Nirvana would be regularly played to a fanatical response. Grunge didn't ever define the music on our playlist at the time, though, but we played a fair amount each week.

Other popular music at the time was mainly indie rock, rap, some film soundtrack music and some heavier dance tracks. The chart stuff at the time included the likes of Right Said Fred, Paula Abdul and Wet Wet Wet, which – for us – was just lame. Wet Wet Wet were playing a gig in the city one night soon after we opened and turned up at the door looking for some late beers. We turned them away, though, and sent them next door because we hated their music with a passion. Marti Pellow et al were more surprised than disappointed, to be fair.

The music equipment set-up at Fifth Avenue comprised two Technics 1210 vinyl turntables plus a twin CD player on top of an old flat piano. We had turntables capable of mixing records, but unfortunately ninety per cent of our DJs weren't capable of mixing – including me. The main issue with our set-up was that it was all on the same level as the main dance floor. This was an issue when we had a full dance floor because if somebody barged into the piano or there was lots of bouncing, then the needle stylus would skip off the record or could skip the CD. A big problem was trying to stop the moshing crowd from crashing into the DJ area and we dreamed of having a proper DJ booth. The dance floor would get feisty and raucous during certain songs and, to put it mildly, people would go flying.

There were a few tracks guaranteed to cause this skipping/ crashing issue, including 'Smells Like Teen Spirit' by Nirvana and 'Kennedy' by The Wedding Present. After I put the needle on the record, I needed to brace myself with my legs outstretched to the back wall and holding onto the piano base, ready for what would happen. As the crowd began moshing to Nirvana, bodies would start flying into the piano. Both Kev and I had to be present to hold the turntable decks steady. At times, we had to drop the song's volume, if the moshing was getting too crazy and it seemed like they'd forgotten the actual track that was playing. As the dance floor got out of control, we'd also need a third person at the front of the piano – nearest the dance floor – to stop bodies flying into the DJ set-up.

It was awesome to have a late drinks licence, rather than finishing at midnight. We were at capacity straightaway and operating a one-in, one-out system from the opening night onwards. It seems like the music Gods aligned and we formed a large, late-night club at the perfect time. Once the indie/alternative crowd had been very separate, but within the space of a couple of years all the mainstream drinkers/clubgoers started to love 'our music', too.

Every new year, we allowed clubgoers to partake in the Peterborough tradition of celebrating at midnight in front of the Guildhall as the cathedral bells rang in the background. People would leave the club and go for a celebratory kiss with a stranger in the open air for thirty minutes and ring in the new year. Some people would couple up on the cathedral square and not return.

Kevin Robinson

Some time ago, I curated a mixtape of tunes, any of which could potentially have been played at the opening night of the Sugar Club. It's impossible to remember exactly which records were in those cardboard boxes I would carry to town each Saturday night (it was a while before I eventually invested in ADDA flight cases), but there were several singles that the indie DJ dared not leave home without in 1991. I'm looking at my slightly dog-eared original twelve-inch copies right now. There's 'Sit Down' by James, which was guaranteed to provide unification on the dance floor among the bowl cuts, Madchester 'cool as f*ck' T-shirts and ridiculously flared Joe Bloggs jeans. There's 'Groove Is in the Heart', Deee-Lite's technicolour collage of P-Funk, jazz, flower-power kitsch, daisy-age hip-hop and disco that even the most stubborn of clubgoers couldn't resist. Then there was 'Loaded', which I'd first heard on a night out at the Laughing Gravy at The Posh Club. I had to ask someone who it was by and I was gobsmacked by the reply. I had no idea about the Soul II Soul drum loop from a bootleg remix of Edie Brickell, or that the dialogue sampled was from a biker movie starring Peter Fonda, and certainly no comprehension of how a jangly indie guitar band like Primal Scream could have created something like this. It was genuinely unlike anything else I'd been exposed to. They had made rock 'n' roll into something more danceable – more euphoric, even – and this would become a key record in terms of where my musical tastes would take me.

There's one track, however, that remains pivotal in the direction that the Sugar Club would take. A few weeks after our inaugural night, I took the weekend off and went to my first Reading Festival. Studying the bill now, it's obvious that I'd spent far too much time sitting around campfires, drinking Merrydown cider, getting stoned and talking complete bullshit, and not as much time enjoying legends like Sonic Youth and Iggy Pop as I'd subsequently led people to believe.

On the first day, I recall a large group of us making our way into the arena to catch a mid-afternoon set by a band called Nirvana, which culminated with the singer hurling his own rather fragile-looking frame into the drum kit. I know I bought *Nevermind* when it was released a few weeks later, then took it home and was blown away by how good side A sounded. There was a level of hysteria about the band that rapidly gathered momentum and within just a few weeks 'Smells Like Teen Spirit' was in the top ten and Generation X had found its spokesman.

The band were playing venues that were clearly too small to contain them (I will never forget seeing them in Nottingham's Rock City). All hell broke loose each time the song was played at our club, so much so that it actually became impossible for us to play it after we had reached full capacity, such was the intense and often violent reaction to it. People would even mount the window ledges and launch themselves off the speaker stacks, and there would be a chaotic mess of flannel shirts, lopsided fringes and flailing limbs all pogoing in unison beneath the chandeliers. To this day, I've never known a record provoke anything like that.

It felt like everything happened so fast back then. Only a year earlier, my schoolmates and I were frequenting The Bell Tavern pub (renamed The Mayfair for a brief period) by the stone bridge in Deeping St James. They promoted indie gigs and I managed to talk my way into getting the odd DJ slot, playing the few credible records I owned in between live sets from local bands with names like 'The Flaming Underpants from Mars' and 'The Dancing Wuli Masters'. I'd been building up my record collection, though. Prior to the days of affordable CD reissues, much of my record shopping was done at one of Peterborough's only alternative shops, House On The Borderland, tucked away from the shiny mirrored gleam of the Queensgate shopping centre and positioned beneath a tattooist at the end of dank alleyway. The proprietors were two slightly bizarre but amiable beardy blokes, who, you suspected, had an encyclopaedic knowledge of the works of Tangerine Dream and King Crimson. Cardboard boxes full of old dusty vinyl were positioned around the walls and in among them lay a treasure trove of obscure sixties garage, psych-rock, prog, punk, goth and psychobilly, in a scene that resembled very quiet but intense chaos. The records were often jammed into the boxes so tightly that you couldn't flick through with any kind of ease, and you were therefore forced to either attempt to identify each record from the top inch of the sleeve alone or lift the whole lot out and run the risk of being unable to return them safely to their home. In addition, an array of flyers, fanzines and Marvel comics lay strewn about the place, alongside clothing, bongs, smoking paraphernalia and an inordinate amount of clutter. There was plenty of material in there for a lunch break's worth of crate digging, plus I could load up on cheap Hendrix and T. Rex vinyl for the Sugar Club. Vintage picture sleeves were Blu-tacked onto the walls and you would generally spend hours rifling through racks and agonising over choices.

I was asked to be involved with the Sugar Club from the beginning in August 1991. I'd worked for Steve Jason on several things since I was at school and I knew Pete Elderkin from his inspiring Laughing Gravy nights at The Shamrock and The Posh Club. They secured a VIP suite with tall arched windows at the top of a building, which overlooked Laxton Square and, until recently, had been used as the county courthouse. Two record decks were placed precariously on top of an old piano and a battered, barely functional till was placed downstairs in reception, where the cloakroom was a flimsy clothes rail buckling under the weight of trench coats and backpacks with band names Tippexed on them. The bouncers didn't know what to make of all the people with brightly dyed hair, spray-painted Doc Martens or scuffed high-tops, oversized shorts and the ubiquitous 'short-sleeve band T-shirt worn over long-sleeve band T-shirt' get-up that would confront them in a queue that stretched down the side of the market each Saturday night. In fact, one cruelly suggested to me that it was a 'night for dropouts'.

Until 1991, Fifth Avenue was probably the most nightmarish of town-centre nightclubs, which Sugar Club regulars would likely have gone out of their way to avoid on a Saturday night, especially if they happened to be walking by at chucking-out time. I'd discovered my copy of *Attitude* magazine from 1995 in which Jarvis Cocker revealed the inspiration behind Pulp's anthem, 'Mis-Shapes'. He recalled being confronted by identical-looking blokes in white short-sleeved shirts and loafers roaming the streets of Sheffield in packs and ready to hurl abuse and violence on anyone who looked alternative or who deviated from their shit-sleep-drink definition of heteronormativity.

Just as we felt like naughty kids banished to the attic, 'Mis-Shapes' was a rallying cry to all the outcasts – anyone who felt excluded, had been bullied or had the crap kicked out of them for not conforming. In a subsequent BBC documentary he described the song as "like all the speccy losers were coming out of the libraries and taking over." Seeing Pulp headline Glastonbury particularly felt like a call-to-arms, that we were winning some kind of revolution, that we would all be returning home to a much brighter existence where Simply Red and John Major would cease to exist. Complete bollocks, as it turned out, but I struggle to name any other bands that have made me feel that way.

Mary Leen Hagger

It's hard to write objectively about the Sugar Club. For a shy sixth former like myself, it opened a whole world in my hometown of Peterborough in 1991. A good proportion of people who had teased or bullied me had left school, which gave me some much-needed relief. I could go on the school bus and into school without a barrage of abuse. It was all very positive and meant an immediate extension to my circle of friends. Some of these friends could drive, so we could go out into town to pubs, bars and clubs. I had a Saturday job at Boots and I loved make-up and as it was just after the eighties, backcombing and hairspray were my thing, as was blue eyeliner. I had been to a commercial club before, where we all wore heels and dresses, but there wasn't a feeling of friendliness. I learnt, the hard way, that a white bra would show up under strobe lighting, though.

In 1991, the film *The Doors* was released. I loved how everyone looked – long hair on the men, and amazing eyeliner! I thought it was the epitome of cool. Once we started going out to the alternative music clubs, I loved how everyone looked. There were girls with black eyeliner and dark make-up. I loved it, but feared it. I realised I would look like a rebel. I tried it out one day and my mum told me to think of others. I removed the black eyeliner, as though it was the sole cause of any selfishness! My rebellion must have lasted for about ten minutes.

I went to indie clubs with my sixth-form friends. Hairstyles for girls varied. The most popular was very long hair with a long fringe where you could gain a bit of bounce in your hair by changing the sides of your parting. Some of the girls started dying their hair with red lowlights/tints with varying success. Clothes varied, but were all black. Whatever the gender of my sixth-form friends, they all wore black. Our clothes choices were influenced by a lovely hippy-style store in Peterborough's Westgate Arcade called 'Rod and Maureen's'. And although we tended to wear jeans, tie-dyed tops could also be seen on a night out!

I really did not like bouncy indie music like The Wonder Stuff's 'The Size of a Cow' or 'Welcome to the Cheap Seats'. Fans of that music wore a lot of colour – for example: James band T-shirts, yellow and purple tops, and outer layers around waists. I assume they wore jeans. I have no idea! It was through these bouncy indie fans that we learnt about the Sugar Club. The Sugar Club was a new club in town, playing alternative music. *Another one*, I thought, but I went along to take a look. The Sugar Club was part of an impressive building. It would continue to be confusing to some people as the main building was shared with a very mainstream huge-capacity club. All we had to do was find the right entrance.

After a long queue, we got in. The entrance area looked very nice and there was a cloakroom and an important staircase!

The club had a nice feel and it seemed clean – believe me, this was important. Yes, it was shared with the less-than-friendly commercial club, but this meant that it had a team of bouncers and felt organised. I really liked the bouncers; they were friendly, which was important as I was needy and wanted a chat while waiting in a queue, even though I was very shy then. Once up the stairs, which took a while, a door opened and there was the scene straight out of *The Doors*. People milling about, looking cool and behaving quite differently to the mainstream club people. No dancing in a circle or hanging around in huge groups, plus there was a real variety of music. We must have stood at the bar, just listening and watching. The music wasn't just bouncy indie – I recognised some sixties tunes. When a break was needed, we would look for an area to lean on (I don't remember needing to sit down!). At this point, there were sofas in the Sugar Club. We could sit on the end or on the back of one if we didn't know anyone on them. It was a time in my life when I would have watched rather than participated.

Steve Jason

We started on Saturday 11th August 1991 and I honestly cannot remember if we filled it to capacity, but it was busy and the initial reaction was 'this is good'. The Fifth Avenue door staff, used to dealing with 'usual clubbers' on the front of the main club were quite taken aback that these people – who may have looked a 'little strange' – were actually quite polite when spoken to… which was a bit of a difference to next door. The big sound system and basic lighting worked well and Pete, Kev and Nathan kept the dance floor full for most of the night, with a mix of alternative stuff from recent years. As far as I can recall, there was nothing 'new'.

The room at Fifth Avenue was basically just an L-shaped room with a bar in the top corner, but it was decorated nicely –

1991 – FIFTH AVENUE KICK-OFF

with decent settees and nice chandeliers. It also had a sweeping staircase leading into the room, so it was a class above previous 'alternative' clubs. The good thing was that nothing was fixed in one place, so every six weeks or so, we'd move everything around just to make it look a little different. Even the dance floor was a wooden 'portable' one, so we moved that around, too. The first week was a success. We even had a lot of Pete's old regulars from the Laughing Gravy nights come down – happy at last to be able to hear alternative music until 2am. How long would it last? I clearly remember Pete thinking it might last until Christmas, if we were lucky. I thought that if we stuck to playing alternative music, and there was no damage to the venue, Howard might be persuaded to let us carry on a little longer.

Then, during the August bank holiday, everything changed when Kev went to the Reading Rock Festival and came back enthusing about a band he had seen causing chaos. He played me the album in the shop and said, "This is the single that's going to change everything." He first played it the Saturday after Reading, so that would have been the first Saturday in September. By the end of September, we had to plan when we played it and make sure we had doormen in the club to look after the carnage it caused on the dance floor. We had people 'stage diving' from ledges onto the dance floor, which was a mass of bodies going bananas. The band was Nirvana and the single was 'Smells Like Teen Spirit'. Grunge had arrived – big time.

I've been involved with music and promoting ever since I was at school. At Deacons, I was in charge of organising the sixth-form socials and saw the punk era emerge in '76/'77. I don't mind admitting I was a 'soul boy' at heart and in '77/'78, while my fellow sixth-formers at Deacons were playing the latest punk 45s in the form room, I was into Jazz Funk and going to the events arranged at places such as The Fleet and The Grove. However, regardless of the genre of music, one thing is clear –

for a 'scene' to exist, it had to have music *and* fashion. They go hand in hand.

On the 'alternative' scene, it went like this:

'76/'77 – Punk
'78/'81 – Two Tone / Ska
'81/'83 – New Romantics
'84/'86 – Glam Hair Metal
'87/'89 – Madchester Baggy
'89/'91 – Rave Era

So we'd really started the Sugar Club at the back end of the Rave/Madchester scene and as any scene evolves, it gets weaker as copycat bands come through, normally signed by desperate record companies who missed out on signing the scene creators. This time, there was a record label in Seattle on the western side of the USA called Sub Pop and the bands leading the charge were Nirvana, Soundgarden and Pearl Jam etc. – and there was a dress code. Suddenly, cut-off tartan shirts, tight black jeans and boots were the order of the day and we had a new generation of eighteen-year-olds (well, maybe a few under-eighteens) coming through, but we had 'a scene' at the club. However, to Pete and the DJ's credit, while it would have been easy to simply just play the current tracks by the 'scene' bands three times a night, they stuck to their policy of playing a wide variation of 'alternative' tracks from all eras. The thinking being that while you wouldn't like every tune played, there would be something you liked played at least two or three times an hour. We were off and running and attracting new people every weekend, as the word spread about this venue in Peterborough playing 'different' music. Christmas 1991 came and went and we were still going strong. There was an enthusiasm in the air as new bands on the grunge scene came through.

Top 10 worst places to live in the UK, from the Daily Mail.

The Shamrock Club, Peterborough

The Pleasureheads

The Sugar Club dance floor

Pete, Kevin and Andy

Michelle and Kristy

Martin and Andy

Mary Leen Hagger

Steve Jason

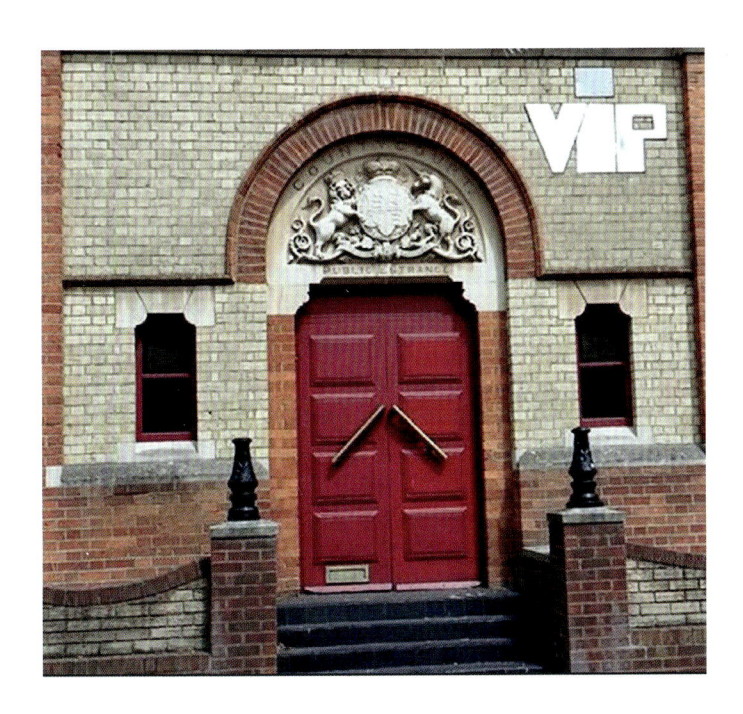

Fifth Avenue entrance

Allen Adams

Metropolis Lounge entrance

Pete

Martin, Pete and Nathan

The chronological line of DJs from day one was Pete, Kev and Nathan from the start, then we had a great guy from Wisbech called Andy, who owned the record shop in the town centre. He used to come with his 'roadie' – Simon, we'll call him. I can recall going upstairs to Andy one night and asking if he had seen him, as a woman had been asking for him on reception. He gave me a look and said, "He's under the piano." Now, Simon liked a drink, so I assumed that maybe he'd had a couple too many and fallen asleep. I looked under the piano and saw him with a big grin on his face as he gave me a thumbs up... and pointed downwards. My eyes travelled further and, although it was quite dark in the room, especially under the piano – which, in essence, was open on all sides – I could see that he wasn't alone under there. In the midst of the darkness, I could see the outline of a woman who, shall we say, was 'looking after him'!

After Andy, I think we gave a few guest slots to a guy called Clive, who was a throwback to the New Romantic genre of the early eighties, with his white shirt and black leather trousers. I think he managed to get away with playing Duran Duran on a couple of occasions before Pete gave him the 'infamous' team talk.

Around this time, I thought we needed to improve the sound system in the club – it had become clear that the people we attracted were, in the main, 'music-led' and not really interested in the usual fixtures and fittings of the 'glitzy' clubs around town, but in meeting and dancing. They were used to going to gigs and festivals and seeing big speaker stacks either side of the stage. I saw a sound system advertised in Liverpool that had previously been installed in the legendary Cream Nightclub – the price seemed okay so, after a bit of negotiation, I was in a van heading towards Liverpool to pick it up. I brought it back to Peterborough and took it to the club. Howard took a long look at the ten-foot-high speaker stacks at either side of the room and said, "F***ing hell, Steve, it's a bloody function room, not Glastonbury!" It worked for the crowd we were attracting, though. The windows vibrated nicely.

1991 music: 'Been Caught Stealing' – Jane's Addiction; 'Come Home' – James; 'Movin' On Up' – Primal Scream; 'Hit' – The Sugarcubes; 'Freak Scene' – Dinosaur Jr.; 'Bring the Noise' – Public Enemy; 'Lithium' – Nirvana; 'Even Flow' – Pearl Jam; 'Wear Your Love Like Heaven' – Definition of Sound; 'Gett Off' – Prince; 'The Only One I know' – The Charlatans; 'Happy' – Ned's Atomic Dustbin; 'The Emperor's New Clothes' – Sinéad O'Connor; 'Shall We Take a Trip?' – Northside; 'Suck My Kiss' and 'Give It Away' – Red Hot Chili Peppers.

Guest DJ Nathan Ciriello played at the Sugar Club at the very start before moving away to Sheffield for university. Our Italian friend had numerous guest slots through the years and still runs the Loaded nights with Martin.

1992 – SPECIAL DELIVERY

Every year, the club's music policy morphed as new people and the latest alternative music came along. There were also a lot of song requests. Some of these were gold dust, like when a great track was suggested that fitted within the music style and kept the dance floor full. However, there were many requests for songs that would clear the dance floor, apart from the requester. Typically, it'd be a hardcore metal track that was requested just at the moment everyone was enjoying some fun, lighter tracks. Sometimes, these 'rubbish' requests were requested on repeat and at a louder and louder volume as the requester got drunker and drunker. This could be exasperating when you explained (politely) that the track would only appeal to one person in the three hundred-capacity club. Sometimes a request might be cool but so obscure that no one knew it or possibly a particularly slow track. There would occasionally be unexpected requests like the one from an attractive woman who asked me to play a song once and then flashed her boobs in my face as encouragement. To be fair to her, it definitely did encourage me and I'd encourage that sort of initiative. Over the hundreds of song requests we had, they were a great way to meet new people and many friendships developed just from their request. Multiple lifelong friendships started at the club and what better connection is there than finding a friend who shares a love of the same music.

I was lucky to be able to get a lot of new releases for free, a couple of weeks before they went on sale. I had to write away and convince the PR company it was worth their while and that our little club was cool and packed with potential indie record buyers. The best alternative/indie music came from a London-based agency called Streets Ahead. They sent us the latest releases from Creation Records, including Oasis, Teenage Fanclub, The Boo Radleys and many others. 4AD records and Mute Records were always super exciting, too, and we could get a lot of mixes that weren't available. About three or four days a week, I'd get a knock on the door in the morning from our local postie, who'd pass me the new twelve-inch releases that'd been mailed and wouldn't fit in the letter box. It gave me that lovely feeling of a birthday morning as a kid when you knew something exciting would arrive for you. I knew a lot of posties well from playing football for the Royal Mail. Sometimes, if I'd left for work early, they would even drop off parcels to me directly at my office desk – you can't beat that for service.

Generally, we'd play new releases and requests in the earlier part of an evening to encourage people to arrive early rather than later when the bars were closed. I got a selection of new alternative releases from Hereward FM, where I was a volunteer playing new releases on the radio each week. I worked with some great DJs, including Paul Coyte, and also did some radio interviews. Bands interviewed included Cocteau Twins and Capercaillie and a bizarre interview in London with Luke Goss (from Bros) who had his shirt unbuttoned to the waist, which felt odd in the daytime. Hereward FM unfortunately changed their music policy after a year and my weekly new music piece was pulled when they joined a new radio network. The music policy they adopted was to play nationwide 'hits' (aka pop releases) with a bland playlist and no room for anything different. It was such a shame that these inane sounds were foisted upon listeners up and down the country, with no regional variations, and it's no wonder that new smaller radio stations started up doing their own thing. The DJs were not even talking to them live or with the listeners, but instead just slotting song intro links into a computer programme. They'd insert digital advert blocks into the software so that a week of shows could be produced in a space of hours at a keyboard. A few numpties got rich producing this sort of radio and they should be ashamed that it proliferates with no originality or local content. There was no spontaneity or reaction to listener feedback, like you get in a live club situation. A club DJ knows instantly what the club thinks of a song choice – people will tell you straight.

While 1992 may have been an *'annus horribilis'* for the queen, it had been a great year for us. Suede were launched onto the scene with 'The Drowners' single and it was the start to an amazing few years of the peak 'Britpop' era. The music was superb and so many classic tracks were being released at the time. The club was going from strength to strength and the music being released was amazing. Some weeks, there'd be half a dozen brilliant new releases. Those songs are trapped in time and feel special. They were great times.

The club also reflected what was happening in the city and a big part of this year locally was about football. The Posh were promoted after a bruising summer play-off evening in Huddersfield in May 1992. I went away to see them play and was lucky to get out safely after a riot occurred after the game, but we had won to get us into the play-off final. Celebrations in our club were crazy at that time, which ended up in a special win at Wembley, just an hour or so down the A1. Whenever there was a football World Cup or Euro Championship, the club would pick up on the mood of the country and play the latest related tracks like 'Altogether Now' by The Farm, 'Can I Kick It?' by A Tribe called Quest or 'March' from *The Great Escape* film.

Mary Leen Hagger

1992 came along and I remember that it was a wonderful time culturally. Music was great and alternative comedy like *The Mary Whitehouse Experience* and *Vic Reeves Big Night Out* was being shown. Personally, it was not the best time, but that had never stopped me before. I went to Germany for the Easter holidays and I noticed that Nirvana had found its way over. The student nightclubs in Germany were very similar to the Sugar Club. Everyone wore what they wanted or, slightly ironically, a uniform of black T-shirts and black jeans. The music was also very guitar-based and, to my delight, moshing to The Clash and headbanging to Nirvana took over the small dance floor. I can't remember when I first 'moshed' or 'headbanged'. Some friends bent over and moved their heads only. I had a bad back (yes, at eighteen), so I tended to dance moving my shoulders and then my head from side to side! The Sugar Club had become the most popular place for the sixth-form set and A5/A6 printouts or flyers were coveted. This ensured a cheaper entrance into the club before a certain time. I also distinctly remember bringing in a small Easter egg, which gave me cheaper entry.

The guys were still growing their hair, the middle-parted 'curtains' – neither long nor short – were being replaced by longer hair for men. For women, perms were (thankfully) being replaced with longer hair or, hairspray permitting, bobs. I had to lay off the hairspray. Personal circumstances had led to me having alopecia so, while I wanted to bulk up my hair to hide my bald patches, it was a losing battle. I remember 1992 as a year of all types of music being played at the Sugar Club. I am sure that it was around this time that an electronica band called Finitribe played there and I remember Prodigy 'On a Ragga trip' being played a lot.

I also remember being sorry to leave the Sugar Club behind when I left home, but mentioning it to some of my new student friends. Coming back to Peterborough for a week in the autumn, and for longer at Christmas, was wonderful. It was decreed that the Tut N Shive was the pub to meet in before going to the Sugar Club. I noticed, around this time, that the Sugar Club was less influenced by its neighbouring club, Fifth Avenue. However, there were the odd, very well dressed – and by this, I mean, conservatively dressed people – who clearly meant to go to Fifth Avenue, but came in the wrong door.

Kevin Robinson

In 1992, I became obsessed with Suede. They had an unashamedly effeminate frontman and songs and imagery that referenced androgyny, chemical highs, violent sex and a then unequal age of consent. They were different to the clichéd bands in flannel plaid shirts, signed in the aftermath of Nirvana's meteoric ascent to stardom. They had many risqué lyrics about life including taking albinos to Heaven on broken bicycles. You didn't really get that with Ned's Atomic Dustbin. To me, it felt like I lived in one of the nowhere places they would sing about – a culturally barren wasteland strewn with cul-de-sacs, flyovers and Happy Shoppers. Places where, for your own safety, you had to go to great effort to conceal any evidence of flamboyancy. They were a band for us – the kind of foppish geeks who were never picked for teams in PE. Their songs were different and exciting; something I could slide into my Walkman and stride around town to with a new confidence. I would stock up on flared cords from Pop Boutique, virtually lived on B&H and even attempted a lopsided haircut that ran across my face and came to rest somewhere near my jawline, thus rendering my right eye incapacitated for much of the mid-nineties.

For me, however, there's no record that sums up 1992 more accurately than Flowered Up's 'Weekender'. It described living solely for the forty-eight hours of pills, thrills and bellyaches at the end of a humdrum nine-to-five working week and then questioned the numb hollowness of the aftermath. They called it '*Quadrophenia* for the Spike Island generation'. I can remember the charts being full of cheap-sounding rave versions of kids TV themes; The Shamen's Dickensian drug dealer, 'Ebeneezer Goode'; chemically enhanced trips to Ferry Meadows with a happy hardcore tape in the car stereo and bottles of Mad Dog 20/20; road trips to Strawberry Fayre where literally any guy you encountered with dreads and a tie-dye top may well have been a member of Ozric Tentacles; and the *Screamadelica* album sleeve being passed around for everyone to snort drugs off.

By this period, I'd got into rave and electronica and was always looking for ways to break up the dominance of indie guitar tunes at the Sugar. I would regularly go to Shock on Friday nights, a rave night at L'Aristos nightclub. At festivals, I'd watch The Orb, where the sound of cockerels and light aircraft would whizz from the left to the right of the PA and their light shows would give the illusion of the entire stage levitating beneath an illuminated sky. Sometimes I'd head to Megadog in London, a sort of hippy-rave on Holloway Road, where body-painted people wrapped in tin foil would wander menacingly through the crowd on stilts and there would be live sets from acts called things like the Psychick Warriors Ov Gaia. I would attempt to introduce the Sugar family to tunes by the likes of The Sabres of Paradise, Aphex Twin and Transglobal Underground. I wasn't always successful, but at least we weren't always playing it safe.

1992 music: 'Midlife Crisis' – Faith No More; 'Plush' – Stone Temple Pilots; 'Mrs. Robinson' – The Lemonheads; 'Twisterella' – Ride; 'Bloodsport For All' and 'The Only Living Boy In New Cross' – Carter USM; 'Big'– New Fast Automatic Daffodils; 'It's On' – Flowered Up; 'Killing In The Name'; 'Know Your Enemy' and 'Bullet In The Head' – Rage Against the Machine; 'No Rain' – Blind Melon; 'About a Girl' – Nirvana.

Guest DJ Danny B was a top man who played hard-core rock, metal and grunge, was a regular guest for a while and wore torch-light glasses on occasion.

Guest DJ Clive was a guest DJ from the early days, played goth and metal music and reminded me of Andrew Eldritch.

1993 – BRITPOP

In 1993, we saw the next level of the Britpop phenomenon and we were there at the very beginning. It was already an electric time for us with so many great bands having releases around the same time. When Suede's debut album landed, it was exciting and a case of the perfect music at the perfect time. Kev was a big Suede fan and he even managed to blag his way into one of their music videos – dancing in bubbles, believe it or not. Blur had been around a while and had some good older dance floor tracks, like 'There's No Other Way', which we'd always played but now they were massive. Likewise, Oasis signed to Creation Records, had BBC radio play and were all over the music papers as the next big thing. I got their first demo, a white label twelve-inch release of 'Columbia', which I played regularly, and their hype was just growing and growing.

Working with Steve as my club partner was always good fun. He generally had about five ideas a week and was never short of new initiatives. In his early days he had been a DJ, playing and building club nights at bars and nightclubs with the soul and dance crowd around the city. He'd also been successful building up his day job of organising music concert tickets and transport, travelling around the UK to see artists like Bowie and Springsteen, progressing to overseas trips like Robbie Williams in Paris. He loved to debate and discuss ticketing or music policy strategies *ad nauseum*. What may start as an innocent aside comment from me about, say, what music works well with clubgoers early in the night could turn into a five-hour monologue as to the correct 'early doors' music policy. A positive was that he was able to jump on the decks in an emergency and keep the dance floor rocking during a 'dancier' slot in the evening, using his mixing skills and experience.

Responsibility for the flyers was his and he had some awesome ideas for amusing ones over the years. Some of the most memorable ones were those that used popular film images, including the *Star Wars* film characters like Chewbacca travelling across the universe, supposedly trying to find our place tucked away in little ole Cambridgeshire. The *Trainspotting* and *Pulp Fiction* films were also popular flyers and they seemed like 'our movies' as they were quite left field but had made it as genuine big-time crossover hits. He also loved to hand out flyers to people on the street and talk to them – he is basically never lost for a word. Somebody would say they weren't into our music and Steve grilled them on what music they *did* like and why, so they needed to be on their toes. I had my mailing list from the LG days and this, added to the weekly names and addresses we'd built up, meant we had a good database. We'd also physically post out flyers to our members.

The Sugar Club at Fifth Avenue had become the stuff of (Peterborough) legend at this point and any alternative music lovers from the area would have wild nights out, getting smashed and dancing with their mates until 3am. We had our turntables and CD players on an old grand piano (lid down), with a metal hoarding at the front. This meant that there was a small space behind the hoarding under the piano, which provided some privacy. When clubgoers found out about the space, it became popular as a place to go for some privacy in an otherwise packed club. It happened frequently that some clubgoers would get amorous, start kissing and then sneak under the (old) grand piano and get carried away with each other. It could be very distracting when you were trying to cue up a track to see a couple underneath, in front of your legs, in various stages of undress. I was announcing something on the mic one night when I glanced down and was surprised to see a couple underneath the piano. A young woman was talking into what looked like a small microphone, but, on closer inspection, I realised it wasn't a microphone at all!

Those nights would usually be raucous affairs with lots of frivolity and craziness. People would dance on the tables and on the raised window ledges, and there could be people passed out or recovering on the floor at times. There was a lot of pleasure and laughing, but maybe a little pain, too. When the house lights came on at the end of the night, it could be like a war scene with shocked, dazed people staggering for the exits. People would stagger down the long staircase, queue up for their coats and then head off, away into the night.

Mel

I first entered the Sugar Club doors in 1993 at the age of seventeen. I fell in love with the place very quickly. *Wow*, I thought, *this is my kind of club and music*. Soon enough, if anyone needed me on a Saturday night, I would typically be in the Tut N Shive from 7 to 9pm, before heading to Sugar. In those days, I loved having the dance floor to myself at the start of the night, but not so much now.

I have such fond memories of the six years between 1993 and 1999, sitting on the stairs but standing when the bouncers came up, meeting friends, dancing for most of the five hours and pestering the DJs to play particular songs. They were six years of my life that I will never forget.

1993 music: 'There's No Other Way' – Blur; 'Cannonball' – The Breeders; 'Laid' – James; 'You Love Us' – Manic Street Preachers; 'De-Luxe' – Lush; 'Everyone's Gone' – Senseless Things; 'Velouria' – Pixies; 'Insane In The Brain' – Cypress Hill; 'Mesmerise' – Chapterhouse; 'She Bangs The Drums' – The Stone Roses; 'Hallelujah' – Happy Mondays; 'Rape Me' – Nirvana; 'Cherub Rock' – The Smashing Pumpkins; 'Rearviewmirror' – Pearl Jam; 'For Tomorrow' and 'Sunday Sunday' – Blur.

Extraordinary resident DJ, Kev Robinson lasted the first six years as a resident DJ with me, a stylish, hilarious, fun, Suede aficionado. He would never be swayed or pressured by requests to play the indie hits and had a take-it-or-leave-it attitude to his sets. If no one was dancing early on in a set, he wouldn't panic and go for an obvious floor-filler. He'd always stick to his guns. He might play Abba next to Suede, next to Nirvana and followed by Deee-Lite, and he just managed to get away with it. He had great magnetism and we laughed so much every night. There was many a night when I was concerned about whether his next choice of track would bomb on a crowded dance floor, but invariably with a 'Who dares wins, Rodders!' attitude, he pulled it off. I met Kev first when he was working in Steve's ticket office and he was always fun – never boring. He left to work in London and we all missed him terribly. We loved him and the place wouldn't have taken off without him. The track that reminds me of him and how great he was at the club is 'Beautiful Ones' by Suede.

1994 – IT AIN'T GONNA HAPPEN

Nirvana was past their peak chart popularity, but had established themselves with some great albums. They were still a major force in our alternative music scene and we'd be playing several tracks by them each week. April was therefore a tumultuous month in our scene because of the shocking news of the death of Kurt Cobain. It was a major event and was spoken about by the world media, even though Cobain still wasn't known by your average person on the street. There were upset people at the club that night. The end of Nirvana marked the end of grunge as a major music force. The shock was palpable and it felt like a traumatic experience among all of the band's dedicated fans. The first Saturday after his suicide was an unusual night; many tribute tracks were played and there was much hugging and crying. It was like there had been a death in the family.

In the same month, we had the first Oasis release, 'Supersonic', the *Parklife* album by Blur and the *His 'n' Hers* album by Pulp. This was the start of Britpop becoming a major music genre and suddenly there were big chart hits to back up all the hype about these bands. It was a strange feeling when the music we loved started to become the fashion of the day in the UK. For the first time, some of the songs we played would get plays next door in the big commercial nightclubs. There was a two-page feature in the local free newspaper and I was quoted in it, explaining the Britpop genre. It felt like vindication for all the indie music fans in an odd way. 'Oh yes, for years you thought our music was rubbish, but now you love it yourself'. I think a part of all of us just liked keeping these bands secret and didn't want them to become 'the norm', but that music was now becoming the mainstream. There was an underdog mentality about our club and indie music fans generally. Many of the regulars had had people taking the mickey out of them or some sort of banter about their left-field musical tastes. So it felt weird, even if only for a short while, to have the same mainstream music tastes as many others. I think it was a feeling that most of us found unusual after years of no one knowing the bands that we'd mention. It did feel like a 'we told you so' moment.

At Fifth Avenue, we were always under the iron rule of the general manager, Howard. He was a likeable, diminutive Northerner with curly permed hair, who scared the staff terribly and would regularly bollock them on the spot. On his nightly round of the club, if it seemed the disorder of our dance floor was getting too crazy, he would say, "Steve, it ain't gonna happen." It became his catchphrase. He came from the seventies and eighties nightclubs of disco and soul, and could never understand us or our music or clubbers, but a dollar was a dollar and we were always busy, so he mostly left us alone. Next door to us, our pal, Paul Stainton, kept the main commercial dance club full to the rafters. He improbably went on to work as a BBC TV sports presenter.

Underage clubgoers trying their luck was an occupational hazard and a constant battle for us, as we didn't want the local law taking away our alcohol licence. The trouble was that everyone was inventive and many had a fake ID, such as their older sibling's birth certificate. As mentioned, one way that we caught out a few of those attempts was double-checking their birth sign. One of our regulars, Carly, said, "I remember Steve J rang my mum once and my mum lied for me... I was fifteen."

Another occupational hazard was the smell of cigarette smoke in the club. When I would get to the club, it'd be a lovely clean large wooden dance floor, freshly scrubbed and smelling pleasant. You would only realise the acrid smoke of nicotine on your clothes and body when you got home. By the end of each night, there was always the smell of stale beer and hours of sweaty dancing, despite the air con being on full. There'd be steam coming off the dance floor as we got busy, with cigarette butts, beer bottles and pint glasses littered around – and that was with glass collectors on the go all night. We would usually have some special on lager, cider or bitter, and these guys and gals were putting them away, so most would be worse for wear at closing time.

Kevin Robinson

By 1994, the Criminal Justice and Public Order Act was passed and raving in the open air became an act of defiance. I'm reminded of the gatefold sleeve of The Prodigy's *Music for the Jilted Generation* album, which folded out into a landscape portrait of a grungy raver armed with a machete, raising a middle finger across a gorge that divided a dark police state of industrial decay on one side, from the sunnier, sound-system-in-a-field generation on his side. Not only did The Prodigy have Peterborough origins, but they were also the ultimate crossover band, equally at home in Castlemorton as they were in Castle Donington. Everyone connected with them, whether you were a metalhead or a fan of Metalheadz, and by the mid-nineties, their live shows demonstrated all the hunger and aggression of rock bands like Rage Against the Machine.

I wanted this level of diversity in the Sugar Club. If you rolled in at 1am, you were just as likely to hear a Carpenters song as you were a Faith No More track or the theme from *Wonder Woman*. The KLF would be rubbing up against Chic on the decks, and people would be rocking out to Anthrax or Fugazi one minute and Josh Wink the next. It's this range that made us unique, at least for the time. Okay, we weren't exactly redefining the traditional disciplines of the indie disco or breaking the mould as such, but we'd certainly rely on our own instincts rather than rigidly adhere to the norm.

Of course, the club had its firm dance-floor favourites, but, looking back now, I cannot think that any other club night could have equalled us in terms of diversity. With the likes of the Utah Saints, The Shamen and Altern-8 on our setlists, we devoted a certain amount of time each week to more rave-orientated tracks. There were also the incredible albums by The Pharcyde, Cypress Hill and the Beastie Boys, and we invited local hero Jonno to play sets comprising largely of hip-hop and acid jazz. Clive would keep the goth contingency happy.

Mary Leen Hagger

It may have been different for other people, but, for me, this time was all about one of my favourite genres: grunge. My heavy metal-loving friends could now join me in the Tut N Shive and the Sugar Club. My hair was also growing back, but it was early days. Some of the indie fans and sixth formers had stopped coming to the Sugar Club. I was lucky enough to go back for every university holiday and meet my friends there, as if nothing had changed.

Looking back, grunge gave less options for girls: our hair was even longer, Doc Martens were more prominent, and we all wore leggings. I paired this look with loose cotton tops and some beads. I had a blue cotton top and, if I was feeling adventurous, I would team it with a long blue skirt with mirrors in it. To give the people of Peterborough their due, I never had any unpleasantness about how I was dressed. For boys, it seemed a little easier. Some were shaving parts of their hair but leaving some parts long. Sideburns were still long and padded checked shirts, when not worn as warm outerwear, were ceremoniously tied around waists to reveal long shorts and big boots.

I loved the music of Faith No More and Pearl Jam. Some moshing instances had led to full-on fights in the Sugar Club, which were terrifying to see. If 'Killing in the Name' was about to be played, I would run from the dance floor. Generally, the Sugar Club was peaceful, though. I was looking forward to seeing it again once I returned from my year studying abroad.

Steve Jason

So we're running along every Saturday, with a constant crowd – normally never less than a hundred and fifty people. On occasions, we'd hit the two hundred mark with a queue outside, especially during the summer and Christmas holidays when students returned to the city from university. It's amazing how fast time flies without you realising and before long, we'd celebrated the second birthday of the club. Somewhere in that time, I booked a bouncy castle for the club – don't ask. The sight of alcohol-influenced people running for ten metres and then diving into an inflatable castle is not normal in a club. How someone didn't actually puke up on the castle is a mystery…

As mentioned, 'scenes' come and go. The first waves of new bands on a scene are the forerunners and leaders, then you get the next wave influenced by the scene leaders, possibly with songs not quite as strong, but they're still hits. Then, you get the next wave of bands influenced by the second wave and, again, the songs are weaker. It's at this point the music papers and radio stations start looking for the next 'big' thing… and it came from

Manchester and, to a lesser extent, Essex. Kev was on the case first, playing me a single by a band from Manchester in April 1994. It wasn't quite as immediate as 'Smells Like Teen Spirit', but with the likes of *NME* and Steve Lamacq enthusing about the band, it was clear something was happening... and it was – big time.

In the space of maybe three months, we went from a club where the clientele were dressed in tartan shirts and black jeans to a club where Fred Perry T-shirts for both the boys and the girls (see the subtle hit single in there), flared jeans and Adidas tracksuit tops. Britpop had arrived. I'd never seen so many Liam Gallagher wannabees in the club. They even imitated the way he walked as they approached the club. The period of 1994 to 1996 really was a peak era for our club night as Britpop took over the nation – and because it had crossed over to the general public, the appeal of the club spread. It was also good for the DJs as anything by Oasis or Blur could revive a sagging dance floor and what made it easier was the fact that both bands had name-checked older bands as influences, so tracks by bands like The Beatles (Oasis) and The Kinks (Blur) could get an airing on the turntables (or CD players).

It was also interesting that, for the first time, you'd hear tracks that we'd played for some time being played next door in the main nightclub – a sure sign of how big the genre had become.

1994 music: 'Their Law' – The Prodigy; 'Bellbottoms' – The Jon Spencer Blues Explosion; 'Love Spreads', 'Ten Storey Love Song' and 'Begging You' – The Stone Roses; 'Dizzy' – Vic Reeves & The Wonder Stuff; 'Come Out And Play'– The Offspring; 'Loser' – Beck; 'Longview' – Green Day; 'Buddy Holly' – Weezer; 'Basket Case' – Green Day; 'All Apologies' – Nirvana; 'Laid' – James; 'Daughter' – Pearl Jam; 'Into Your

Arms' – The Lemonheads; 'Tuesday Morning' – The Pogues; 'Supersonic' – Oasis; 'Rocks' – Primal Scream; 'Sabotage', 'Root Down' and 'Body Movin'" – Beastie Boys.

Guest DJs Kristy Homza and Michelle Butt were inseparable guest DJs who'd be in the club every Saturday. They had a strong following and great style, leaning towards harder rock/metal. Cool and hard-hitting.

1995 – MIS-SHAPES

'Mis-shapes, mistakes, misfits
Raised on a diet of broken biscuits, oh.
We don't look the same as you,
And we don't do the things you do,
But we live 'round here, too, oh really.
Mis-shapes, mistakes, misfits,
We'd like to go to town but we can't risk it, oh
'Cause they just want to keep us out.
You could end up with a smack in the mouth
Just for standing out, now really.'

The lyrics of the awesome song 'Mis-Shapes' by Pulp neatly sum up the feelings of what it was like to be into indie/alternative music in our area during the eighties and early nineties. Our people dressed differently and liked different music and seemed to think differently – not better, but different. There used to be risks associated with wandering around looking a bit different or standing out from the crowd. After a few years, though, it became a lot safer for our clubgoers on our streets and the strength in numbers helped.

This was, undoubtedly, Pulp's year with two massive hits

and Jarvis Cocker becoming an icon, fifteen or so years after his band started out. Pulp were the headliners at Glastonbury this year and cemented their position at the pinnacle of Britpop bands with a seminal performance that raised their profile even more. Now, though, the tables were turning and the often-derided music was taking over the 'proper' mainstream music charts. The local newspaper rang up a couple of times asking me to do articles explaining the Britpop music scene. Things were starting to change.

In August, we had the Blur versus Oasis Britpop singles battle when 'Country House' by Blur and 'Roll with It' by Oasis were released in the same week. The national press got everyone excited about the bands and we had new people trying to come to the club every week. The Britpop genre was only ever a part of our playlist, so if anyone wanted a whole evening of Britpop, they wouldn't find it at our place and they'd hear a much bigger mix of music.

There were some fantastic crossover dance/alternative, big-beat releases this year, including 'Life is Sweet' by The Chemical Brothers, 'Born Slippy' by Underworld and 'Santa Cruz' by Fatboy Slim, all of which were rocking the dance floor. The club dance floor was loving the heavier rock and dance crossovers like the Big Beat genre. We tried a couple of gigs at the venue, like the dance act, Finitribe, but we found that it took too long to get the band gear out and get the club ready after the show, so we just focused on the music rather than live acts.

An urban myth started to develop around this time. It concerned a young, attractive woman who had supposedly come to her demise in the club. In the Fifth Avenue venue, after the entrance and cloakroom, there was a long staircase that went around the edge of the spiral stairs until it reached the door to the club. As you opened that door into the main area, there was a blast of music and the heat would really hit you. At the landing before the entrance, there was a five-metre stretch that would get congested with clubgoers coming out for the toilets and new arrivals trying to get into the club. At the top, if you look over the long, black metal balcony rail, it would be a drop down of about seven metres, enough to induce vertigo. The story was that as this woman was sitting on the handrail and leaning backwards with her legs in the air, she was accidentally bumped. She went flying backwards, did a somersault and landed flat on her back. It was rumoured that she broke her back and it had been hushed up, and that she never recovered enough to visit the club again and passed away some time later. Either way, people started to move very carefully in that balcony area and it coincided with the door staff upping their efforts to keep the stairs clear.

Towards the end of this year, the sad death of a rave clubgoer also shocked the clubbing world. The eighteen-year-old died in Essex after taking ecstasy and quickly drinking lots of water. The profile it raised nationally was big and there was suddenly lots of interest in what happened inside UK nightclubs. While some of our clubgoers undoubtedly took drugs, Steve and I did what we could to prevent drug dealers selling in our club. The staff of many clubs knew that drugs were sold inside or just outside their venues, but we were both quite anti-drugs and there was already enough craziness inside caused by alcohol.

Louise Hartje

The Sugar Club – oh, the memories! I went there from 1991 for many years. I worked at HMV at the time and was good friends with Kev Robinson. My memories include kids always getting told off for dancing on the windowsills and the god-awful settees that were dotted about the place, and it was always a rush to get one. My friend, Susan, and I were always the first ones to get in and always stayed until the end. I used to hound Kev to play The Lemonheads and he would start the night off with them. There was another DJ who played New Model Army and other bands that I was not keen on and Nathan sometimes DJ'ed, too. There was Jonno from Market Deeping, as well, and him and Nathan played The Wonder Stuff, Pop Will Eat Itself, Mega City Four and other bands like that.

I loved walking up the stairs to the room as it was the only place for alternative/indie music on a Saturday night. The bar was tiny in the corner. I remember an older small guy always came on his own and everyone knew him. He wore chinos, a shirt and a jumper, and danced all night. I never spoke to him, but he loved to dance. I lived for Saturday nights. It was such a cool place to go; I made a lot of friends and met my former husband there, too (maybe not a good memory).

The playlist really broadened my knowledge of music. I still listen to the playlist Kev made on Spotify. I might be wrong, but I am sure there was a student night or a cheap weeknight that started in Fifth Avenue and they opened the door to the Sugar Club and that is how I discovered it, though I could have dreamed that bit. The place was always bouncing by midnight and it was the best place to be on a Saturday. 'Linger' by The Cranberries would be one of the last songs played before the harsh lights came up at 2am.

Martin Rowe

If my memory serves me well – and let's be fair, whose does at my age? – I started my playing at the Sugar Club on Saturday nights in 1995. I was at college, working part-time in an independent record shop and already DJ'ing on a Thursday, at a student night in Boston, Lincolnshire. The Sugar, however, was where I wanted to be. To jog anyone's memory that needs it, the Sugar Club did not look like a club. The wide spiral stairs led you up to the main room (the VIP Suite at Fifth Avenue). The room itself was like a dining room of a stately home, with a chandelier, high ceiling and large windows with big window ledges. You were greeted by a small bar; a wooden dance floor surrounded by a few tables and chairs; two moving "disco lights"; a grand piano with a mixing desk, a pair of 1210s and CD decks on it; and a big f***-off sound system. That was it and it was perfect.

My friend and DJ'ing partner, Andy Sutton, was already playing regularly at the Sugar and I was introduced through him. I was booked as a 'break beat' DJ for my first night and laboured over a record bag of what I thought were clued-up tunes from reputable labels like Bolshi, Skint, Tru Thoughts and Junior. I played an early set; after four or five songs, I was asked to "Play something with some f***ing guitars in, please." I dove into a CD box and pulled out some Charlatans, maybe some Levellers and Elastica. It seemed to do the trick. After my set, Pete Elderkin put his arm around me and said, "F*** 'em, I thought your set was great. Are you busy next Saturday night?" I was in.

The mid-nineties was a time of real change – artistically, politically and, best of all, musically. Music defined who we were and who I was. I don't think I've ever had a meaningful relationship that hasn't, at its core, been strongly linked by music. It was tribal and you could tell if someone was your kind of person just by what band T-shirt they had on. Saturday nights in the mid-nineties were fuelled by alcohol, drugs and music. The Sugar was a safe space for outsiders – those of us who were glad that we weren't welcome at clubs like Fifth Avenue.

The freedom we had as DJs was incredible. Think about it: where else could you play Ananda Shankar, Korn, Elvis Costello, Frank Sinatra, Lo Fidelity Allstars, Deus, N.W.A, Belle and Sebastian, Sonic Youth, Rage Against the Machine, Shirley Ellis and the Bonzo Dog Doo-Dah Band, all in one night? It was awesome and the crowds gave you the freedom to try to find something new, because they were with you.

When it comes to guitar music, The Sugar had started during the grunge era of alternative music. By the time I joined, it had transitioned into what came to be known as the Britpop era. Music and bands that had been underground were now becoming more mainstream and more radio-friendly, and the lines between pop, dance, indie and hip-hop were becoming less pronounced. I think this is why it was such an exciting time to be playing music in a club. The rules were dissolving. Old songs that were now springing up from film soundtracks were big floor-fillers. DJs had their own styles and their own personality when it came to some choices, and many of the songs being played on BBC Radio 1 were uplifting, positive and very much about enjoying the moment. Bands like Pulp, Blur, Oasis, Supergrass, Primal Scream, The Charlatans and Suede were driving this love of alternative music into the mainstream.

There was also incredible music coming from America. Beck, the Beastie Boys, Eels, The Breeders, Hole and the Smashing Pumpkins all got weekly plays. I retained my love of playing dance/break beat, too, so artists like The Chemical Brothers, Underworld, Fatboy Slim, Daft Punk and Leftfield were permanently in my record bag – and yes, a record bag! Getting the chance to play and mix with vinyl was a real love and treat for me, even on busy nights when the chances of the needle slipping were very high.

1995 music: 'Leave Home' and 'Life Is Sweet' – The Chemical Brothers; 'Common People' and 'Mis-Shapes' – Pulp; 'I'm A Believer' – EMF, Reeves and Mortimer; 'It's Oh So Quiet' – *Björk*; 'Connection' and 'Waking Up' – Elastica; 'Tonight' and 'Bullet with Butterfly Wings' – The Smashing Pumpkins; 'Charmless Man' – Blur; 'This Is A Call' – Foo Fighters; 'Time Bomb' – Rancid; 'Queer' – Garbage; 'Begging You' – The Stone Roses; 'Buddy Holly' – Weezer; 'Just When You're Thinkin' Things

Over' – The Charlatans; 'Caught by The Fuzz' and 'Alright' – Supergrass; 'Being Brave' – Menswear; 'Inbetweener' and 'Swallow' – Sleeper; 'Aeroplane' – Red Hot Chili Peppers.

Guest DJ Andy S had a legendary DJ pairing with Martin from out of town. He was reminiscent of the Nirvana frontman with his bleached locks, but he always had nicer jumpers. A larger-than-life character, a great man to spend time with and a consumer of alcohol at times. He ran his own record store, reminiscent of the *High Fidelity* film with John Cusack, but his store was in Wisbech, not Chicago – Lisa Bonet never visited his store. I remember he'd play a great mix of modern tracks from the likes of The Verve and The Charlatans, mixed with classics like 'I'm a Man' by The Spencer Davis Group and 'Sympathy for the Devil' by The Rolling Stones. One evening, after a few years working together, we had a particularly crazy time and the following Saturday he never returned, vanishing into thin air – having partaken in too much partying was the rumour.

1996 – FENLAND BERMUDA TRIANGLE

The club seemed to morph and renew its membership every year with the next group of kids and the next new music to be added into the mix. Britpop and all our great music were now mainstream and shows like *TFI Friday* had just started on Channel 4 with BBC Radio 1 DJ Chris Evans hosting. It had great groups playing and it was filmed live in London, so I really wanted to visit the show and applied for some tickets. *Trainspotting* – the Danny Boyle film – was also released, which was awesome, and the club took it to their heart, loving the dark humour and the brilliant soundtrack. Songs by Iggy Pop, Lou Reed, Underworld and Sleeper from the soundtrack were all regularly played during a night.

One regular fixture of DJ life then was that you needed to lug heavy boxes of twelve-inch and seven-inch vinyl records around. I had a one-metre-by-one-metre CD case, two heavy twelve-inch album flight cases and a smaller box of about a hundred seven-inch vinyl singles. You needed flight cases to protect the records and to stop beer spilling into them in the DJ booth. At set-up time, about 8pm each Saturday, you had the option of two trips from the car, invariably in the rain, or you could go crazy trying to lug it all up in one go. The issue with doing it in one go was that you had a long set of stairs to negotiate, and you'd probably go head over heels. If you lifted half of the load at a time, it was easier to do, but then you also had to keep an eye on the floor below in case some smart-arse tried to pinch the records as they walked past them towards the local pubs.

It was also zero fun making the trip backwards at the end of the night, trying to get to your transport. As well as the cold, icy or wet weather at 3am on Sunday mornings, you had to walk past hundreds of drunken clubgoers milling and messing about after all the local clubs turfed out their punters into the street at the same time. Sometimes there'd be a fight going off and you'd have to try to negotiate yourself past safely without drawing too much attention to yourself. Drunken clubbers insisting to see what records you had and wanting to critique your collection was to be avoided. Then, once safely in the car or the cab, it'd be off to the local Turkish takeaway to queue up for a doner kebab. After that, it was home for the *Match of the Day* recording and a couple of beers to unwind. Generally, it'd be a 4am/5am bedtime and then up for Sunday morning football at 9am.

Indie music had become very linked with football over the last few years, with TV shows like *Fantasy Football League* connecting to our crowd. While a lot of our clubgoers weren't really 'into football', it was a fun time and Baddiel and Skinner – hosts of the show – were 'alternative' comedians from the early days who just stayed with 'us'. Baddiel and Skinner teamed up with Ian Broudie for 'Three Lions (Football's Coming Home)' – the ultimate party song for on a packed, hot evening at the club during the Euro Championships in 1996. This classic song was played twice a night in our club during those weeks. Another one of 'our' bands was New Order, who released the classic 'World in Motion' football song, which was a dance-floor favourite.

This was also the year when a few rumours started to circulate, which took the club to a mythical status. One of these concerned the missing DJ Andy S, who, after being a regular jock every Saturday for three years, apparently went missing after a big evening at the club. The story goes that he was travelling home after our club and was lost in the Fenland Bermuda Triangle fog somewhere between the towns of Crowland, Wisbech and March. He was never seen again. His record store was closed and there was only an occasional rumoured sighting. At that time, hardly anyone had a mobile phone, so communication was a problem. It was hard to confirm many of these stories, as although the internet was around, it cut out at Wisbech, which is allegedly too dangerous for non-locals to visit to check. Les Ferdinand, the former England striker, who played non-league football for a while, said that it was the most intimidating place that he'd ever played. We'll never know what happened to Andy. It's a mystery.

Kirsty Mulhern

I can't remember what time of year it was, but I wasn't wearing many clothes, so maybe it was the warmer months. It was a usual Saturday at the Sugar Club's Fifth Avenue venue, with Steve Jason on the door and everyone moaning at him about how long they'd had to queue for. There was a sweeping staircase and balcony at the top, and a good chunk into the night and several pints in, I was sitting on the balcony, as everyone did, chatting to John Mulhern (who I'd recently started dating) and Gary Meadows. John went to the loo a floor down and Gary said something that made me laugh. Here, it gets technical…

I was at the start of an eating disorder (thankfully a short-lived one) – which didn't affect my drinking capacity, oddly – and I was very thin. I wore these massive, heavy platform boots and as I laughed, tilted back and raised my feet a bit, my centre of gravity shifted and over I went. All I remember was waking up on the floor with Lisa McKeogh looking over me, very panicked. Johnny had emerged from the loo to see his girlfriend flying past, so he was also pretty panicked. Apparently, I had blood trickling from my mouth and everyone thought I was dead. Paramedics were called and insisted I stay on the floor (I really thought I could get up and rejoin the party upstairs). I was ambulanced off to Peterborough District Hospital, where I spent a couple of days.

All I sustained from the fall – which was a drop of at least twenty feet onto hard concrete – was a fractured hip. A bit of a non-injury, but I still walked with crutches and sticks for a good six months afterwards. The doctor – and this has been my mantra for years – said that beer saved my life! Had I realised what was happening and tensed up, I'd have probably broken my neck or spine, but, as it was, I was still laughing at Gary's joke when I hit the ground. It didn't occur to me to sue the Sugar Club or anything like that, and I'm glad I didn't. Steve Jason gave me free entry for life and that was like winning the lottery!

I loved it there – a mixed bag of punters, but everyone knew everyone. It was just what you did on a Saturday night after Bogarts. Very fun times.

Steve Jason

We were really 'rolling with it' during this period and enjoyed full houses most weeks, sometimes hitting capacity by 11pm, with a queue of people waiting to hear the door staff shout, "Two more!" as two people left. I think the whole country was in a 'Cool Britannia' moment – there were occasions when Pete would be playing a bootleg version of N.W.A meeting Oasis's 'Wonderwall' and then you'd hear the same song being played next door!

However, being packed so early often brought its own problems – people come early, people drink more and they… need the loo more. On many occasions, we suffered the "Toilets flooded!" shout as we were on reception. This usually meant running into Fifth Avenue and looking for a glass collector to come and unblock the toilets – from memory, it always seemed to be the ladies' loos that suffered the most. Pete would be upstairs in the main room, totally engrossed in looking after the music, while it would be left to me on the front door to try and solve the problem of water flooding out of the toilets – all good learning for later years. There was also the infamous glass collector who managed to 'look after' a lady behind one of the speaker stacks and then an hour later was seen entering the ladies' toilets with her best mate. You'd think the guy had had the best night of his life until it was reported back to Howard, who promptly dismissed him for 'not doing his job properly'.

To be fair, Pete was always on the case with the music. In football terms, you could say he was the 'holding midfielder'. He was quite happy to let Kev be the 'flamboyant striker' by leading the way with new bands and new singles, but if the floor was slipping, then it would be Pete who would play the dance-floor favourites to ensure normal service was resumed. The only 'non-negotiable' music-wise was that no metal music should be played by anyone, even it was requested. I think on one night, there was a new DJ who had told Pete he had a great following. Note to any DJ reading this and wanting to get a break in a club: promise the promoter that you've got twenty-five people wanting to hear what you're going to play and you'll get an audition. However, if you get it, then you must deliver the people. Anyway, I was on reception that night and I heard the intro to Metallica's 'Enter Sandman' start to reverberate through the sound system… and that was it. After no more than thirty seconds, silence. Then, Pete's voice boomed out over the PA,

"This is the Sugar Club; we don't play any f***ing metal here," and an indie banger immediately took its place. I don't think that DJ was invited back.

However, on the other hand, it wasn't all full-on alternative tunes for five hours on a Saturday night. People may think it was the likes of the Chicago Rocks club or maybe Flares that led the way with the 'Abba Revival'… nope, it was us. On reception one Saturday, it was a 'WTF moment' when we heard the intro to Abba's 'Dancing Queen' coming out from the upstairs room. I think the doorman (we only ever had one doorman, as Howard usually needed them all next door) looked at me and I looked at him with a "Who the f*** is playing this?" I went upstairs and two hundred pissed-up alternative kids were singing at the top of their voices. I think Kev may have discovered/realised his calling, but it was all good. Other notable 'Sugar Party' faves were The Carpenters' 'Top of the World' and a 'rave' session that would often end up with 'Take Me (To Infinity)', causing havoc on the dance floor or on the window ledges.

Unlike today, where trying to find a young alternative DJ with a finger on the pulse of what alternative eighteen- to twenty-one-year-olds are into, music-wise, is just impossible, we had a lot of people asking us for slots. I used to pass them over to Pete. His audition would be: 'How many mates have you got into this music?'

As we moved towards 1997, the Britpop era – like every other 'era' before it – was weakening and we saw a shift to a more 'dance-orientated' scene, with bands like The Prodigy, The Chemical Brothers and Stereo MCs coming to the fore. I think Andy Hilders had joined Pete as second DJ around this time and between them they adapted and rode out the new wave of music. As mentioned, Pete's philosophy was to simply play a bit of everything to keep most people happy. But it was also noticeable that there was a 'harder', rockier sound also coming through.

Bands like the Red Hot Chili Peppers were certainly making their mark on the major festivals of the time, but we were not really noticing any other bands beginning to emerge on our side of the Atlantic.

Martin Rowe

In early 1996, I took an unplanned break due to having meningitis. It kicked the shit out of me and nearly put an end to me. Luckily, it didn't and, after maybe three months, I felt well enough to start coming out again. Things meant a bit more to me than they used to after that; I tried harder with my song choices, looked harder for something new and different, took a few more risks with what I played (not always to Steve's liking) and, most of all, felt so pleased to be back among, what I could call, 'my people'. At a time when I was struggling to adjust back to normal life, the Sugar gave me a safe space and something to look forward to.

As the decade moved on, I was doing pretty much every Saturday night as a resident DJ. We welcomed in more guests like Andy H, Danny Spence and Marcus Day, all of whom brought their own style and musical taste to the Sugar. Occasionally, Kevin Robinson would drop in and show us all how it's done – what a guy. Throughout all my time as a DJ at the Sugar, I had day jobs in record shops: The Record Store in Wisbech, HMV in King's Lynn, and Virgin Megastore in Peterborough. What this meant was I always had a direct line to what was coming out, what was popular and how to get hold of it. I spent so much money on new music to play, I don't even want to think about it. I also used to get 'promos' – pre-releases of new music. I remember distinctly dropping 'Phat Planet' by Leftfield for the first time. I'd nabbed a ten-inch promo while the tune was still being used on the Guinness advert. It went down a f***ing storm.

1996 music: 'Beautiful Ones' and 'Trash' – Suede; 'Lovefool' – The Cardigans; 'Novacaine For The Soul' – The Eels; 'You Oughta Know' – Alanis Morrisette; '1979' – The Smashing Pumpkins; 'She Said' – Longpigs; 'Slight Return' – The Bluetones; 'Devil's Haircut' – Beck; 'Girl From Mars' – Ash; 'Hey Dude' – Kula Shaker; 'Daydreamer' – Menswear; 'Wake Up Boo!' – The Boo Radleys; 'Ladykillers' – Lush; 'Trainspotting' – soundtrack.

Extraordinary resident DJ/musician Martin Rowe did the second half as my co-resident DJ for six years. He brought in and mixed more dance styles into the club. He had short, dark hair, chiselled features and was relentlessly positive. He had an encyclopedic alternative/dance music knowledge, was an ex-record store staffer from the Wisbech crew and always kept the dance floor rocking. We had a couple of hundred evenings together and he was fun, bright and decidedly cool. He always had a plan of his set in his mind and he'd always make it work.

1997 – DON'T LOSE THE TICKET

It was an uplifting year in the UK generally and this was reflected in the club. It was just prior to the Labour Party and Tony Blair being elected in May 1997, and there was a great optimism around the fact that the Conservatives would soon be kicked out of government after more than a decade. We had a local connection to John Major, who was the MP for Huntingdon, and it was a great feeling to kick the legacy of Thatcherism into touch. Many clubgoers had also been on the 1990 poll tax march and we were always a left-leaning club who were happy to talk about it on the microphone. These were the days when DJs did speak a bit during the night and weren't the silent mice-type of DJs that never say a word or connect to their audience. We always loved playing 'Tubthumping' by Chumbawamba, a song against the section 28 anti-homosexuality law, which came out this year, and we'd also play any of the other big protest songs like 'Free Nelson Mandela' by The Special AKA.

It was also a special time in the UK because all 'our' bands seemed to be becoming mainstream and the commercial chart acts were being pushed out of the way. It was long overdue. The city had a connection to one of those big game-changer groups, The Prodigy, who released the classic *The Fat of the Land* album this year, with classic singles like 'Breathe', 'Smack My Bitch Up' and 'Firestarter', which would all send the club mental. They had the perfect punk ethos, big dance beats, killer guitar and unique vocals, and made one of the most controversial UK albums ever. Gizz Butt from seminal local punk band The Destructors became The Prodigy's live guitarist and was an occasional club visitor (we even did his wedding reception disco). The other successful musician that our city produced was our Welsh mate, Spike Smith, who visited from time to time, eventually becoming the drummer for Morrissey, Killing Joke and New York Dolls.

One of the toughest, most unsung jobs at the club was the entry point and cloakroom attendant job. Steve J was the main man and had constant banter and chat with the punters. When we were struck by sickness or people turning up late, it was a job nobody wanted to do. I had to do it on many occasions. Ideally, you had to have two sets of hands to take the right money and give the change, take the coats and jackets, and then pass on the (correct) cloakroom ticket. On many occasions, if someone was sick or late, I'd have to step in and do a shift until reinforcements arrived. Sometimes you had to turn people away because of a drama previously, so you could be unpopular. Entering the club was a rush until we reached capacity and then it was one-in, one-out. But when the club closed at 2am, you were suddenly mobbed with people, in a rush, demanding their jackets back waving their cloakroom tickets. Over the time at Fifth Avenue, we first had Michelle and then Claire who helped on the doors with Steve.

I came home from the club and was winding down with some beers on Saturday 31st August. Just before 5am, the TV news announcer cut in and confirmed that Princess Diana had died in a car crash. The following Saturday, there was a national funeral in the morning and the club was open that night. It was such an eerie, odd evening. Most of the clubgoers weren't royalists by any means, but Diana connected to everyone as an outsider and there was massive love and respect for her. The track that summed up that unusual, subdued evening was 'She's a Star' by James, which I recall made some people cry on the night. It was a weird time and we had a shocked club, with no one knowing quite what to feel.

Kevin Robinson

I guess I must have played at around three hundred nights at the Sugar Club. My journey ends in June 1997, which I suppose followed the inevitable demise of Britpop. Having been its target market, I now detested its descendance into the flag-waving, Loaded, Cool-Britannia farce it had become and how conservative most of the music ended up being. I felt I'd lost my way somewhat with the club and was genuinely confused as to what we should be playing. I was still discovering amazing new music, but most of it wasn't exactly primed for the indie dance floor.

Looking back, I feel privileged to have played a small part in the success of the club. It provided me with a space to grow up and earn a bit of cash for playing some incredible music. It was genuinely thrilling to be a part of it and I shall always be grateful for that.

1997 music: 'The Impression That I Get' – The Mighty Mighty Bosstones; 'Block Rockin' Beats' and 'Setting Sun' – The Chemical Brothers; 'Walkin' on the Sun' – Smash Mouth; 'My Mate Paul' – David Holmes; 'Karma Police' – Radiohead; 'Brimful of Asha' – Cornershop, 'Breathe'; 'Smack My Bitch Up' and 'Firestarter' – The Prodigy.

Guest DJs Pat Unwin/Joe Berridge were guest DJs with eclectic tastes, but funkier than the other DJs. They were into trip-hop, hip-hop and acid jazz among others. Pat was slim and tall – looked a bit like Fatboy Slim. Joe was shorter and smartly dressed in Fred Perry tops. He was also part of a crew of about fifteen lads who used to cause mayhem everywhere they went, whether out drinking or at the football. They both always seemed to have a smattering of young women following in their wake.

Guest DJ Dave Allen was at Laughing Gravy and occasionally Sugar Club nights at the Met Lounge. A tall, lean man with Northern connections (Bolton, I think). A childhood friend from Fletton, who started out as a new wave guitarist and became a great DJ and introduced more of a dance mix to the club.

1998 – TFI FRIDAY

It was another great year of music releases and a warm summer. Maybe last year was the beginning of the end, but 1998 was definitely the end of Britpop – and, as we always did, we just moved onto the next thing. 'Thanks, it's been great, but the music is not going to stop'. New great music continued to turn up every week. The club was packed from 9pm to 2am, with a queue around the block.

There were a lot of great (and some not-so-great) relationships started at the club for various people. In my experience, you can directly improve your chances with the opposite sex if you're DJ'ing, as there is always a natural reason to talk to someone who is asking you to play a song. After a fun chat with someone attractive, I occasionally heard the words that I dreaded, "Shall we go dancing now?" I'd always preferred to just go 'standing' in a nightclub… with a bottle of Stella Artois, ideally. I'm terrible at dancing and don't especially enjoy it, and a great thing about DJ'ing is that you never actually have to do any dancing yourself. Instead, I would be very happy in the squashed DJ booth, singing and dancing and loving the music alongside other people to, say, 'Leave Home' by The Chemical Brothers and its repeated lyrics. I would dance there, but not on the dance floor, where my lack of rhythm was obvious and visible for all to see.

By now *TFI Friday* was having an audience of millions on Channel 4 and a memorable day for me happened one balmy summer in August. I had been wanting to go to this live music TV show for ages and I finally managed to blag six tickets. It was always filmed at Riverside Studios in Hammersmith, so we went on a lad's day trip to West London. What could possibly go wrong? Well, quite a bit, as it turns out. First off, we started drinking at about 9am on the train from Peterborough on the forty-five-minute journey.

The group was made up of the Thursday night football and drinking team: Mitch, a tall, lean man from Norfolk, aka Mitch the Switch, whose cutting wit kicked in after three or four pints; Bon had strawberry-blond hair, hilariously quick banter and came from South Yorkshire mining stock; Gallo had a dark, lean complexion with shoulder-length hair – a former Goth and current Spurs fan; Crossy was one of those sickeningly good-looking men with an immaculate head of dark hair, who was liked by everyone he met; Geordie was a storyteller of epic proportions, with a love of boxing and socialising – he was from County Durham and quite hard to understand, even before he started drinking.

Lunchtime was spent in Covent Garden, drinking and enjoying the sunshine. By admission time at the studios, about 5pm, we were all smashed (well, I certainly was). In retrospect, it may have been a good idea to call it a day then, but obviously we didn't and my recollection from here gets hazy.

We queued up to get into the venue and then as we reached the front door, the security staff reckoned that the venue was full (although, most likely, they just knew we were far too drunk). As you can imagine, this didn't go down so well as we were primed to see the bands and hear them play live. The doormen said we wouldn't get in, but we decided to just wait around and see what happened. The door staff began to get worried when we didn't move and threatened to call the police if we didn't leave the door area. They said we'd need to move anyway, as the musicians needed access to the studio and they were in a dressing room across the road. I then have a recollection of Lenny Kravitz (he's quite cool) followed by All Saints (they're quite attractive) having to squeeze past us to get through the door. Eventually, the door staff called the police and two Metropolitan Police officers arrived. They were obnoxious and cocky, and told us to go away or they'd return and physically move us on. As it was a baking hot day, they were wearing their short white-sleeved uniform shirts. Five minutes later, the police returned. As they walked back towards us again, I vaguely remember asking, "Has someone round here rolled an ankle and called an ambulance?"

These coppers had big egos and this comment obviously annoyed them a fair bit as one pulled out his handcuffs straightaway and the other took out his truncheon. The shorter, stocky one then threatened to arrest my mate, who said, "I doubt you'd be able to do that, mate." True enough, the cop then struggled to handcuff him, as my friend kept his arms spread apart and the cop wasn't strong enough to put the cuffs on both wrists.

A couple of the drinkers outside the pub opposite, who were watching the spectacle in the sunshine, came over and told the police to relax, but to no avail. At that point, the other copper started swinging his truncheon and one of the lads kicked it out of his hand which knocked him backwards over the low wall behind him. They radioed for help and, within a few minutes, a vanload of eight policemen turned up. Using plenty of force, they eventually arrested four of the lads. The Met Police are famed for their 'no-nonsense' approach and they certainly didn't disappoint. In retrospect, though, even factoring in this drama, it was still a great adventure in the capital, 'meeting' some music stars and creating a lot of priceless memories. Met Police 0: The Posh 1.

Mary Leen Hagger

1998 heralded the year of the Superstar DJ and my return to the Sugar Club, when I was back in Peterborough. This return was traditionally governed by the university holiday timings of Easter, Christmas and October. The Tut N Shive was still a place to meet up pre-Sugar Club along with The Solstice, which, at one point, hosted comedy nights. I remember listening to the *Urban Hymns* album by The Verve on repeat at the beginning of the year. There was lots of energetic dancing at the Sugar Club. Both 'The Rockafeller Skank' and 'Praise You' by Fatboy Slim, along with the singalong track 'Leave Home' by The Chemical Brothers and slightly less energetic dancing to 'The Bartender and the Thief' by Stereophonics and 'My Favourite Game' by The Cardigans. I also recall dancing in a big friendly group to the football song 'Vindaloo' by Fat Les for the World Cup. Peterborough was still a very good night out and I remember friends coming to visit.

The Sugar Club fashions were varied. Both men and women sported short hair. Big, clumpy shoes for the ladies, along with halterneck tops. It was still very much a mod look for the men, who sported polo shirts, jeans and trainers. Some were into the skater look with loose-fitting clothing. This may also have been influenced by a love for hip-hop. Sugar Club fans had always been open-minded with their music genres.

1998 music: 'Closing Time' – Semisonic; 'Bitter Sweet Symphony' – The Verve; 'Celebrity Skin' – Hole; 'Sunday Shining' – Finley Quaye; 'Oh La La' – The Wiseguys; 'The Dope Show' – Marilyn Manson; 'My Hero' – Foo Fighters; 'Perfect' –

The Smashing Pumpkins; 'Vindaloo' – Fat Les; 'Take California' – Propellerheads; 'Intergalactic' – Beastie Boys; 'Pure Morning' – Placebo.

DJ Mr Clubman, aka Mark Goodliff, was an amazing dance DJ, totally out of our skill league in terms of mixing records, to be frank, and he did some great guest slots from time to time at Fifth Avenue. He worked at HMV records back in the day with some of our other mates and would mix for DJs at the big commercial clubs.

DJ String, aka Lee, had wild hair, nice guy and a dance DJ who played a mix of styles. We'd worked together and I'm not sure how long it took to read, but he was always carrying the *Mr Nice* autobiography by Howard Marks.

1999 – THE METROPOLIS LOUNGE

This was a massive year for the club as we moved from our home at Fifth Avenue to its permanent resting place at the Metropolis Lounge on Bridge Street in September. The Metropolis Lounge was just a few hundred metres down the road. The advantage of the move was that Steve owned the new place and this meant complete control of the club, the door staff and the whole environment. We had about three 'last nights' at Fifth Avenue, I recall, as there were delays before we eventually moved the club in September 1999. The new nightclub was based up a set of narrow stairs on Bridge Street in central Peterborough, just opposite Woolworths. We now had a 'proper' DJ booth overlooking the dance floor instead of it actually being on the dance floor, which was a luxury for us. We had all our decks, CD players and volume controls/lights all together and a raised bench for CDs and vinyl cases. You could comfortably fit three people in the booth, but sometimes we had five or six squeezed in, chatting and playing around.

The new venue was a hit and we had a huge queue outside the club every Saturday night, almost right up until 2am. Martin was the resident DJ with me and Andy Hilders was there most weeks. I gave a lot of guest slots to people who wanted to give it a go. However, someone new would come and ask to play every week and it was getting hard to give everyone a chance. Some guests were great straight off and others took a while, particularly if it was new to them, as they had to work out the mechanics of the gear and get used to it. I did try to include people whose taste I personally may not have liked, and we tried most new alternative or indie music genres as they appeared. I sometimes asked to know what they'd play if I gave them a gig and I'd get a list of tracks the following week or a CD burned with songs. This showed it wasn't just a drunken request to play and they were prepared to do some work.

We even had a secret entrance for some close friends of the club, like Bogarts bar staff, and they would climb up via the fire-exit stairs on St Peters Road. We did this as it was always hard to get close friends into the club via the front door, as they had to get past a swell of queuing (potentially grumpy and drunk) people, introduce themselves to the door staff and then hope that someone had remembered to put them on the guest list. It's a long, embarrassing journey back to the back past all those queuing punters if you've bowled up to the front announcing, "I'm on the guest list!" However, perhaps you weren't on the list because a drunk DJ had forgotten to add you to it – that was fairly likely.

Those same backstairs were also sometimes the scene of much low-level kissing and making out. To get there, though, the participants would have to avoid the door staff, open the emergency-exit doors and slip into that quiet area on the stairs. Those metal stairs weren't a romantic place, but it was a more private place than the main club. I recall my own brief raunchy liaison on the steps one evening – not quite 18-rated, but it was way sexier than you might imagine. Maybe steps could be the way forward, although I've never seen an Ann Summers shop with a folding step stool in the display window.

At this time, our new club was rocking. We were loving the freedom that came with Steve being in charge of the building and staff, which made life a lot more fun. We were getting so busy that we even opened his balcony area up the stairs at the top of the building, which could fit about fifty more people. We had a different sound room at the top of the venue with a different DJ and tracks playing, as you couldn't hear the main club. We called it the VIP room, although I can't recall anyone famous ever being in there, apart from Chris Turner, The Posh manager, once. After a packed night of dancing and drinking, we would inevitably get to the evening's close. At 3am each night, we played the last song of the night and then it was time to retrieve your belongings from the new hire, Allen, in the cloakroom, find your pals and stumble into the night to get a takeaway kebab or burger on the way home. The only problem clubgoers might have experienced with him was his gruff exterior – heaven help you if you forgot your cloakroom ticket, as you would be waiting to retrieve it until the last clubgoer left the building at 3am.

Allen was Peterborough punk rock royalty, having been a founding member of The Destructors (and the awesome Destructors V years later). They released several records and were banned from venues in Peterborough when punk rock was frowned upon by the local council. He looked after the front of house entry/cloakroom for all the Met Lounge. He would often have long chats with staff and clubgoers throughout the night and he was knowledgeable about pretty much every topic. He was still releasing music regularly and was a mentor for wannabe rock stars of the future. He was a massive part of the Sugar Club in its new home and was even an agony aunt for some clubgoers.

In August, I took a weekend break from the club and went up to Scotland for a music scouting trip. I went to an indie club in

Glasgow to get some new music playlist ideas and onto Greenock to see a friend. I was advised to be cautious on our night out there, as the town was 'the murder capital of Scotland'. The local bars were packed and rough, so for self-preservation, I was advised to order drinks in a Scottish accent to not bring attention to myself. A soft English accent (and bloke) was never going to be popular there. In the end it was a great time, the tall ships race was happening, and the town and the people were awesome.

Steve Jason

Without even really thinking about it, we'd run a club night for over seven years, and it was still going strong. Around halfway through the year, though, Howard called me over. He said that his bosses had been looking at revamping the whole building as they were also reaching their capacity on most weekend nights. The only way they could increase the capacity of the main room would have been to knock the dividing wall down between the two rooms, so, in effect, we would lose our room. Nothing was set in stone, but it made me think about what we would do if they did make the decision.

The answer was to buy my own club and I knew just the one. Having been on the club scene in Peterborough and beyond since the late seventies, I'd seen several clubs come and go. I'd also seen enough layouts to know what makes a successful club work. I also knew that the boss of Winners, Brian Winner, had been suffering with ill-health and was looking to sell up if the right offer was forthcoming. The venue had been Peterborough's first 'proper' nightclub when it opened as Anabelles in 1976, we think. It had had heady days when getting dressed up was the order of the day. Jackets and ties for the gents and dresses for the ladies. In 1983, it had been purchased by ex-Posh boss, Noel Cantwell, who revamped it and renamed it Canters – I DJ'ed there on Sunday nights for three years in the mid-eighties. In 1989, Noel sold out to Brian Winner, who, again, refitted the club and called it Winners. I'd also DJ'ed there on Saturday nights in the late eighties, so I knew the layout of the club. I also knew that although the club itself had a bit of a 'poor' reputation around the town, the dance scene wasn't exactly known for its 'whiter than white' reputation. I also knew that the most important thing about any club is its clientele. While some of our clientele may have looked a little 'strange' to some, they were the best crowd in town.

Protracted discussions with Brian Winner continued over a few months, but the deal was eventually agreed and the contract was set to take over on 25th July 1999. For the first few weeks, I learnt the mundane things such as how to change a barrel of beer and how to ensure you had enough staff to look after the demand at the bar, while also listening to five hours of house music every Friday and Saturday night. Pete continued to look after the Sugar Club, but everyone knew it was a case of *when* we would announce the closing of one club and the move to the new venue. This was one of the key points in the decision to financially commit to a permanent venue. It's one thing rocking up at 8.30pm on a Saturday night, going home at 2.15am and leaving any issues behind, but quite different to have to work on things full-time when you own the venue.

We ran a piece in the local paper about moving venues and I think there's a picture floating around of Pete and the rest of the DJs walking out of the VIP Suite with their record boxes under their arms. The Met Lounge sign went up around the end of October. The reaction to the first night of The Sugar was overwhelmingly positive and instead of waiting thirty minutes to get served a beer at the old place from an overworked bar member, you now had two bars on different levels. It wasn't a 'room', but a properly designed club. You couldn't see everyone in one view, but you could walk round the club and discover a different area – the basis of how any well-designed club works.

Mary Leen Hagger

1999 came round and nu metal was popular but, to be honest, I don't remember if it was played in the Sugar Club. I remember more energetic dancing to 'Hey Boy Hey Girl' by The Chemical Brothers and less energetic dancing to 'Scar Tissue' by the Red Hot Chili Peppers. A few friends had stopped coming and we were heading towards the age of twenty-five. There was speculation in the press about a Y2K bug, in which all computers would malfunction after 31st December 1999 and this would supposedly be solved by inputting all four digits of the year.

Speaking of the 'end of an era', I remember the last night of the Sugar Club in Laxton Square. The beer festival was on so we got to the club quite late. Someone had brought some bubble mixture in and was blowing bubbles. My friends took some pictures and then had them printed in black and white. The song 'Drinking in LA' by Bran Van 3000 was played that night. In the song, there's a comment about the fact that they are twenty-six and it alludes to a regretful heavy night of drinking. It all seemed quite apt and a little bit sad.

I remember wishing other people well. I don't think we knew where we would spend our end of nights in Peterborough. Maybe not straightaway, but many years later, I felt nostalgic for the Sugar Club. It was only eight years of my life, but it was the growing up years and the making of lifelong friends. The fact that it was so full of regulars and a little bit small made it feel safe. Then, of course, there was the music – and what wonderful music it was! I've never found anywhere like it since.

Martin Rowe

I remember the last night at the VIP Suite well. It felt like a celebration of everything that had gone before. Drinking champagne from the bottle, incredible music, familiar faces and old friends. I believe I might have (I definitely did) take an ashtray with me at the end of the night. I was the last to leave the room that night – the place meant so much to me. Unbeknown to me, my future wife was there that night, but we didn't meet until a bit later. The last song I played at the VIP Suite was the first song I played at the Met. I guess I'm a bit sentimental like that.

The early days at the Met took the same spirit and crowd with it. Misfits, outsiders and a love of incredible music. Tastes morphed a little over the next few months – more punk/pop punk, metal and rock were taking the place of the Britpop of the mid-nineties. As much as I still enjoyed playing and seeing a full dance floor bounce in time to the songs we played, I felt more disconnected with the music. The millennium eve night was great fun and I was so proud to be seeing in a new century with Pete, Steve and lots of like-minded people. I made a playlist of three or four songs (on minidisc!), complete with Big Ben chimes, to play at midnight so that we could all be together as Y2K dawned.

1999 music: 'My Own Worst Enemy' – Lit; 'Scar Tissue' – Red Hot Chili Peppers; 'All Star' – Smash Mouth; 'Why Don't You Get A Job?' – The Offspring; 'Celebrity Skin' – Hole; 'Steal My Sunshine' – Len; 'My Favourite Game' – The Cardigans; 'Pure Morning' – Placebo; 'Body Movin'' – Beastie Boys (Fatboy Slim mix); 'Faith' – Limp Bizkit; 'Teenage Dirtbag' and 'A Little Respect' – Wheatus; 'Learn to Fly' – Foo Fighters.

Guest DJ Carla had some slots early doors at the Met Lounge, blonde bob and Doc Martens, grunge and metal music style.

Guest DJ Elm was a fan of ska punk music and Newcastle United, with a warm, enthusiastic personality. A key person on the scene, who knew everybody and played a lot of sets for us.

2000 – SOUND OF SILENCE

At the start of the new millennium, there were stories of digital issues that would grind power grids and the like to a halt. In the event, nothing happened like that, but at midnight we all celebrated the new year as usual. We had a larger upfront admission ticket price and then it was free drinks all night. This meant that, psychologically, punters felt obliged to get hammered to get the maximum value out of the higher price tickets, which they did. Either way, it was a great night – the club and DJs alike were loved up, drunk and the dance floor was rocking.

We were one of the first clubs in the city to get a 3am music licence, so we got an extra hour of dancing (although the bar still closed at 2am for last orders). Sometimes it would mean that the club would fill up a bit later in the evening. We would play the new genre of nu metal and rockier music in the 9–10pm slot – music that had a more limited appeal. I liked to give lots of new DJs a chance to play and that time slot meant we could expand the appeal of different alternative music. This was a year when the music seemed to change again, as it did every few years, and the rockier music was proving more popular. We generally avoided playing much metal as even though that did have an audience, it alienated a lot of people, too. We liked to play a few tracks of one genre at a time, then move on, so that our regulars knew that even if they disliked a particular style of music (say alt rock or Britpop), they wouldn't have to wait too long before something they did love came back on the decks.

One good test of a potential DJ's indie/alternative music knowledge was to have 'Cannonball' by The Breeders playing and then see how they reacted at two minutes, eleven seconds. It's uncommon to have total silence in the middle of a song – at a club, when you get that sudden silence for a few seconds, most people are surprised. DJs check no one paused their music and dancers think there's been a big mistake and look up at the jock. You need a nonchalant, confident smile of someone who knows their classic records and that the song will resume three seconds later. The other test would be the absolute classic floor-filler, 'I Am the Resurrection' by The Stone Roses, when the song stops dead for four seconds at five minutes, twenty seconds. Another challenge for a prospective DJ is whether they can have a pint of lager in one hand and headphones squeezed on the left ear, tucked into their shoulder, then cue up a track with their other hand and take a request.

Initially, we'd had nicely painted toilet doors and facilities at the new Metropolis Lounge club. But after having to remove graffiti and replace broken toilet door locks almost every week, Steve decided to make everything 'unbreakable' and metallic. Even the main toilet mirrors were changed to a reflective mirror-like metal, so you got more of a hazy distorted reflection of yourself, as through a door spyhole. It was a shock sometimes to see people looking worse after a visit to the bathroom to sort out their appearance after a spell on the dance floor. It was often thought that the Sugar Club toilets would be one of the safest places to be in the case of a nuclear war breaking out. They were commonly thought to be bombproof and NASA did call Steve once to see what material we were using.

One of Steve's oddest ideas related to toilets was to have a woman in the ladies' loo, handing out sprays of cheap perfume and hand cream, like an upmarket American bathroom attendant from the early sixties. Unfortunately, there weren't too many cocktail dresses being worn at our place and it was less like *Mad Men* and more like 'Surprised Women'. Safe to say, it didn't catch on with our crowd, who just felt it quite odd for an older person to be hanging around the toilets.

The most popular drinks in the club at this time were probably Newcastle Brown Ale and 3VB (treble vodka and cloudy lemonade) and we would sometimes have a promotion on cheap dry cider in cans – that stuff could make you shudder. Some of the DJs drank heavily when they were working, but, mostly, we just had a couple of drinks to get us in the groove. When drinking, you may feel that you're performing the most amazing DJ set ever, but invariably it was average. The dance floor is the only true barometer of how well you are doing and if it wasn't packed at peak times, then you weren't doing a great job. End of story. The big issue for me if I drank was trying to get the next track queued up ready in time before the current song finished. First off, you had to think of the track you wanted to follow the current one, then you had to find the track that you wanted. Next, you're searching through a couple of boxes looking for it, as the clock counts rapidly downwards. Then, just as you are cueing up the track to play, with five seconds left to go, somebody taps you on the shoulder and wants to request a track at the same time. Pressure.

Steve Jason

Attendance was good and we were filling to capacity every Saturday night. The change of venue had given the club a new shot of energy, but there was a new genre of music coming through fast that, to be truthful, blindsided us because neither

Pete nor Andy had been big fans of the genre. The dress code signalled a new change in the direction of music that was taking over as *the* alternative choice for the next generation of eighteen-year-olds. Suddenly, every Saturday was filled with both males and females wearing the same clothes – well, not physically, but from behind you sometimes couldn't tell who was who. Big, baggy black jeans and a red or black hoodie with either Korn or Limp Bizkit or Deftones in bold letters across the front and, if you were super cool, a red baseball hat worn back to front, ala Fred Durst.

For the first time, I think the DJs struggled to keep the floor working. Whereas in the past they could play a bit of everything because the audience was so varied, the nu metal movement was now so big that on a Saturday night, eighty per cent of the crowd were into it. So, it wasn't a problem to fill the floor – simply stick on a nu metal record – but the issue was that the bands concerned hadn't made that many records, so after playing thirty minutes of the aforementioned band, you'd run out of nu metal records to play. If you then tried to play something from previous Sugar years, such as Oasis or Blur or The Stone Roses, for example, you'd clear the floor as the nu metal fans just walked off and there weren't enough fans of other genres to replace them. However, to their credit, Pete and Andy stuck to their guns and played records that the Sugar Club regulars had loved in their time as the 'new generation', even if the 'energy' of the club dipped for a few minutes. But it was important because it kept the 'bloodline' of the alternative club going. It would have been all too easy to simply have played nu metal music on repeat all night, but then what would happen when nu metal had had its time – you had no night left.

Some of the nu metal tracks could be a little 'hard on the dance floor', to be blunt – tracks like Limp Bizkit's 'Rollin'' would cause major mosh pits to occur and the door staff – who previously were more used to dealing with 'pilled-up' dance fans – now had to learn how to look after a dance floor where people seemed to be 'fighting' but weren't. I recall getting a letter from an unhappy customer, who suggested we should consider putting foam over the barriers that surrounded the dance floor, as her friend had been pushed into them the previous week and was still nursing the bruises.

One of the joys of owning my own club was that I was the licensee – thus it was on my head if any underage person was found drinking in the club. Previously, at the VIP Suite, it was a case of 'Underage? Not my problem!'. To be fair and honest, we've all done it – ironically, I was sixteen the first time I went to the club I now owned, so I was hardly one to judge, but the law is the law and we had to be seen to be following the rules. I think at one point, we were turning away around thirty per cent of the people that arrived before 11pm for either not having ID or having a fake ID. There was a girl who literally lived in the same street as me, who was getting in every Saturday with an ID that said she was eighteen. It was only when one morning I was out walking our dog and I saw her getting into her father's car to go to school that the alarm bells rang. The following Saturday, a closer inspection of her ID showed that either she was in year thirteen or the year of her birth was two years out. It was the latter and she was banned for two years. Sorry, Cherry.

We saw fake IDs of all descriptions – some quite good, some terrible. Some were even borrowed. You'd be presented with a driving licence where the picture looked nothing like the person offering it as ID. So, the trick was to ask another person in the same party what the name of the person presenting it was? Amazing how the person proclaiming to be called 'Adam' on his driving licence, for example, was known as 'Phil' to his friends. My head doorman hit on the idea of asking a person who didn't have any ID their date of birth and noting it. He'd then ask for their phone and ring their mum or dad to double-check it. Ninety per cent of the time, Mum or Dad would confirm the correct day and month... however, they'd be a couple of years out from the year of birth. The person who was proclaiming to be eighteen would actually be sixteen or seventeen. This idea worked a treat until we realised that some clubbers were priming their parents for the 'phone call'.

But overall, the Sugar Club was going from strength to strength. We had a new home that everybody liked – sure, there was the odd moan from the 'older crowd' who would reminisce about the 'charm of the VIP Suite', but, overall, the bigger club had a better layout. More bars appealed to more people. In fact, I'm quite sure that had we stayed at the old VIP Suite, the club would never have lasted as long.

In this new decade, there were two new genres of alternative music coming through as the interest in nu metal began to cool down. On one hand, you had the likes of The Strokes for the 'indie kids' with a dress code of 'skinny' everything; on the other hand, you had the punk or pop punk of the likes of The Offspring and Green Day, which also had its own dress code. Pete and Andy were into the indie style and, luckily for us, a young DJ from Market Deeping said to Pete that he had lots of mates that were into pop punk and could he have a slot? Shaun Phillips joined the team and the club was the strongest it had ever been, full to capacity nearly every Saturday with an enthusiastic crowd who wanted to hear new records.

2000 music: 'All the Small Things' – Blink 182; 'She's In Fashion' – Suede; 'Rollin'' and 'Take a Look Around' – Limp Bizkit; 'Song 2' – Blur; 'Last Resort' – Papa Roach'; 'Good Fortune – PJ Harvey'; 'The Real Slim Shady' – Eminem; 'One Step Closer' – Linkin Park; 'This Is Love – PJ Harvey.

DJ Andy Hilders was working at the club for a few years and it was a bit like having Jim Morrison or Oliver Reed on the decks, such was his capacity for drinking and physical mayhem. He'd invariably been drinking for several hours when he turned up to play at 11pm. All that Dutch courage (ironic, as he's of German descent) made for some inspired music choices from time to time, which he pulled off, inconceivably, and he became one of the most popular. Steve would often try to reprimand him for being the worse for wear, but it was like trying to tell off a puppy.

2001 – TENSION

The year started off positively enough and I looked forward to every Saturday night. In June, the Labour Party won a second successive term in government and we were happy about that – the dark days of Thatcher's years were slowly being forgotten. I met a Kiwi woman who visited my nightclub; she requested some obscure tracks (which I didn't play), but we started chatting anyway. The problem was that although she spoke English, it was a mumbled Kiwi version of English that you couldn't understand, particularly in a noisy nightclub. There was always a three-second time delay as I tried to decipher her incomprehensible accent back into Peterborian. It was worth it, though, and we started dating soon afterwards.

Her four friends never seemed to show any interest in visiting our beautiful city from where they lived in London. They were doing their 'OE' (overseas experience), which often means Kiwis living together with friends from their NZ primary schools, meaning they didn't meet many UK locals. However, I remember her friends visiting the club one time, unexpectedly. It was on the weekend after the 11th of September terrorist attack on New York. For them, I think our city seemed a safer place to be than the capital in the days following the attack. On that evening, they kept asking me to play 'Prisoner of Society' by an obscure (to us) Australian skate punk band, The Living End. As I wanted to please them, I forgot the first rule of a club DJ, namely to keep the dance floor busy, and I threw caution to the wind. Unfortunately, as I played the track, the whole dance floor emptied out in a couple of seconds. The most surprising thing was that even the Kiwi women themselves then didn't want to dance to it on their own. The whole club was just standing and staring at me, wondering what the hell I was playing. Ouch.

Sadly, there were a lot of tensions in our city around that time. Local Muslims were targeted after the 9/11 attacks and a gang of British Pakistanis killed a young white man who worked at a local city bar. It was a hard time and tensions were high around the city nightlife, though a high police presence helped to keep things in check. We had no race issues at our place and we just tried to keep positive and encourage clubbers to book taxis home at the end of the night, rather than traipsing home across the city. Over time, the situation calmed down.

In October 2001, Apple unveiled the iPod and the idea of fitting a thousand songs onto a device rather than lugging around four boxes of flight cases was very appealing. Music was about to be transformed, but it was for personal listening really, so it didn't change what we were doing at the club where we still had a mix of vinyl and CD. I bought a 'shockproof' twin CD player, which made life easier. Now, the occasional slam of bodies into the DJ booth from below no longer caused an issue, unlike the Fifth Avenue days when we were on the same level as the dance floor and holding onto the decks for dear life.

Richard Grange

Although I was a relatively late regular frequenter of the Sugar Club (1997–2001), like many things in our formative years, it has left me with many, many fine memories. At a time when clubs were very much pigeon-holed (rock club, dance club, Hitman and Her club), the Sugar was a broad church. The clientele varied from goths and punks to classic Adidas Samba-wearing indie kids, something that was reflected in the music, too. Where else could you hear The Mission, followed by Nick Cave, then P J Harvey, all rounded off with The Jackson Five? Sure, we all had our favourites, but the real beauty of the place was that it was a club where we could listen and dance to the music we were buying at Our Price or Andy's Records (Christ, I feel old now!).

Memories will always remain and although it was over twenty years ago, it still feels like yesterday. Don't sit on the stairs; don't climb on the windowsills; no, I don't take requests; and no, you can't have a pint of snakebite and black. Holding in a piss was imperative owing to the state of the gents – that's if you could get in there, as on many an occasion an amorous couple would be locked together in a drunken embrace! Grabbing a seat was also impossible – far better then to retire downstairs to the sofa and debate and discuss events with Steve Jason and the much-missed Allen Adams. A conversation with the latter was never anything other than interesting...

Sugar Club myths abounded. One centred around someone falling from the balcony but not breaking any bones; another of two lads jimmying the door in the corner open and getting into Fifth Avenue. Most legendary of them all, though, was that you could get served at the bar in under fifteen minutes and make it back to your table without spilling beer everywhere. I had the pleasure of working on the door a few times for Steve. Putting aside the lack of change ("Got any pound coins, mate?") and the bunfight that was the cloakroom at kicking-out time, they were great times. I'm not sure how much money I cost Steve from letting mates in for half price, but I'm sure he'd forgive me.

Great friends were made. Many have long since vanished, some are sadly no longer with us, others regularly crop up in conversation with my wife (she was a Sugar regular, too). It would be remiss of me to start naming names – suffice to say that if you knew Simon Stabler, you'd have known me, too. What stands out most for me about the Sugar Club, though, was the atmosphere. I never once saw a fight, never once had any aggro – although at six feet four, that was rare anyway – and instead was surrounded by people who were all after the same thing: a brilliant night out.

Martin Rowe

At the club one night, I met the woman I would marry just over a year later. I'd seen her throughout the night and she eventually made her way to the DJ booth and asked for a song. I was praying that it wasn't going to be shit and, of course, it wasn't. The Sugar Club was where our lives changed. Our love of alternative music is what brought us there and something that continues to be a constant in our lives. Twenty-two years and two teenage children later, we're still going strong – listening to alternative music, buying records and going to gigs. I often wonder how different it all could have been had we not met at the Met. In 2001, with life moving on, more commitments, age and location meant that I felt the time was right to hang up my headphones. It was the right time and it signalled the close of a period of my life that had been so much fun.

2001 music: 'Drive' and 'Wish You Were Here' – Incubus; 'No One Knows' – Queens of the Stone Age; 'Bleed American' – Jimmy Eats World; 'Fat Lip' – Sum 41; '1979' – The Smashing Pumpkins; 'Control' – Puddle of Mudd; 'Clint Eastwood' – Gorillaz; 'Bohemian Like You' – The Dandy Warhols; 'Hate to Say I Told You So' – The Hives; 'Hash Pipe' and 'Islands In The Sun' – Weezer.

Guest DJ Phil was a polished DJ/musician and a wiry, fun, smiling guy, like an alternative Tom Cruise but with an East Anglian accent. He was an immediate hit when he became a regular, and he always came up with some great throwback gems from a loved older album.

Guest DJs Robbie and his posse DJ'ed for us several times. He was from out of town, good fun, popular and added a mix of new styles.

2002 – THE PEOPLE, THE PEOPLE, THE PEOPLE

This was another great year for music and we were still going gangbusters, but it was time for a change. I had an opportunity to try something that had not even been on my radar and it felt like the right time. In spring, I decided on a massive change and to take a career break and arrange to move overseas to New Zealand once a visa could be approved. While everything I needed – namely my family, friends, the club and my football team – was here, I was dating a Kiwi and wanted a change of scene and an exciting new challenge. I broke the news to Steve and together we planned a big going-away night.

The bittersweet final night at the club was in June 2002 – I think it was June, but it may have been July. I was presented with some cheap fizzy bubbly to celebrate the occasion on the night. Steve is not prone to extravagance, so I think the bottles he bought, which tasted like a mix of Babycham and Asti Spumante, were his way of saying how much he really cared. That wine really did bring a tear to my eye that night. At about 1am, in the packed club, the music was paused and he did a flattering thank you announcement. Everybody in the club cheered for a full ten seconds… and then the next track was queued up and off it went. Boom, it was all over and there was no going back. The moment was gone. That's when you realise that you're simply a steward, looking after everything and keeping it going until the next person takes over from you. Andy Warhol said we all have 'fifteen minutes of fame', but I reckon it's down to fifteen seconds now and you've got to accept it and move on.

There were so many fun, great people who passed through our place, and a few particular characters spring to mind:

Giles went to my secondary school, but was a couple of years below me. I don't think he'd mind me saying, but he was a little geeky-looking when he first arrived. I remember he came with a briefcase for his books, which meant he endured a bit of bullying by kids in the playground. But seeing him again several years later at the club, he'd come into his own and he was a giant of a man (physically and as a person), with his own crew. He was built like a brick shithouse and could be intimidating in his goth/industrial-style piercings, dreads and tattoos, but you'll never meet a more caring geezer. He was involved in the hardcore rock Planet of Sound gigs in the city, which had a big following, and liked doing loads of weird and eclectic stuff.

Simon was about eighteen years old, six foot tall and skinny, but dressed like an old-time punk rocker with Doc Martens, a ripped T-shirt and braces on his trousers. He would request music non-stop, dance like crazy pogoing to songs and generally be up to all sorts of schemes. He did get a DJ slot once, too. Once you met him, he was never forgotten.

We had the twins, Bridget and Sally, who came to the club at both venues every week religiously for all the time I can remember and always danced the night away with their friends. They both had dark, longish hair and great, engaging smiles. Their music requests would generally get played as I quite fancied one of them at the time and we had similar musical tastes and got on well.

There was a man called Alan, who came to our club from when it started in 1991. He seemed a lot older and wiser than everyone there, and was quite short and bespectacled. Once he started dancing, he would dance in his unique style for the whole night. We feared that lives would be lost in the process, but, seriously, he was just into the groove and enjoyed the dancier tracks that we played. He was great fun and became best buddies with loads of people, and was a regular during our time at Fifth Avenue.

I'll always regard my time organising and DJ'ing at the Laughing Gravy and Sugar Club as a privilege. The chance to be part of so many exciting, fun times for our clubgoers and friends was amazing. We made it into one of the longest running club nights in the UK, playing alternative music every week. We were doing this music well before Nirvana/grunge, and then Britpop changed the music landscape and became mainstream for a while. We provided a place for new DJs to play their favourite tunes and a place to dance to new releases that weren't in the other bars and clubs. We had some great DJs that helped us at the Sugar Club over the years at both Fifth Ave and Met Lounge nightclubs. We had several resident regulars every Saturday night between 1991–2002 including Kevin Robinson, Martin Rowe, Andy H and Andy S. We also gave loads of guest slots to hear different alternative and other styles, and to add more input to the atmosphere. Among the guest DJs that spring to mind were Nathan Ciriello, Dave Allen, Jonno Wyatt, Robbie Neal, Pat and Joe, Steve J, DJ String (Lee), Alex Elmer (Elm), Danny S, Martin D, Michelle, Kristy, Sean, Mark Goodliff, Carla, Daniel S, Shaun P, Phil R, Marcus and loads more.

Most of all, it was a place to socialise, be part of a community and have freedom of expression every Saturday night. So many great nights and events happened in those clubs for our people, who wanted somewhere to hear the music and see the acts that you just wouldn't find in the other bars and nightclubs at the time. The Māori proverb '*He aha te mea nui te ao, he tāngata, he tāngata, he tāngata*' translates as 'What's the most important thing in the world? It is the people, it is the people, it is the people'. The Sugar Club wouldn't have lasted so long and become one of the longest-running nightclubs in the UK without those great people. The longevity doesn't automatically make it a good club, but it's a good indicator. Don't forget that if no one turned up to the club or stopped going for more than a month or two, we would have closed very quickly like most clubs do. When the club's gone, people will realise the importance. Mainly, though, no club will make it without fantastic support and we have the awesome Sugar Club family to thank for that. In English culture, we like to be modest, but every thirty years or so it's okay to pat yourselves on the back. So, thanks to everyone who came along, made new friends, added to the atmosphere and made it such a great club.

The Sugar Club is now synonymous with alternative music in the area and I did my bit from August 1991 until July 2002. Eleven years in Peterborough.

Steve Jason

In early 2002, we were in the office sorting out everything for the night ahead and Pete broke the news: "Steve, I gotta tell you, I'm off to live in New Zealand." I was financially involved with the club so I was going nowhere. So, after eleven years, the partnership of Pete and Steve looking after the 'alternative club scene' in Peterborough ceased to be. We'd started a night that we thought might last a few months (if we were lucky) and it turned into a 'Peterborough Clubbing' legacy. We'd ridden through grunge, Britpop, big beat, nu metal, pop punk and NY indie and lived to tell the story.

Martin Rowe

The way things happened, I didn't get a formal 'last night' playing until my good friend, Nathan Ciriello, contacted me eight years later in August 2009 about doing a reunion night called: 'Do you remember the first time?', which came from a Facebook group called 'Sugar Club Survivors'. We have done several since, at the City Club and the Met Lounge, some with Kevin Robinson, and some with Pete. This meant I did get to have my night that felt like a 'last night' and it was really cool. Nathan and I still DJ under the name 'Loaded', playing a mix of nineties alternative bangers, dance, hip-hop, grunge, Britpop and lots more. It's great to see some familiar faces still dancing to the tunes from the Sugar Club days and it's a wonderful reminder of the last days before the internet, iPhones and social media, where we were the same as the people we played for and we all came together on a Saturday night in Peterborough. It was f***ing ace.

2002 music: 'Get Off' – The Dandy Warhols; 'The Middle' – Jimmy Eat World; 'Smooth Criminal' – Alien Ant Farm; 'Last Nite' – The Strokes; '19-2000' – Gorillaz; 'Yellow' – Coldplay; 'Fell in Love with a Girl' – The White Stripes; 'The Real Slim Shady' – Eminem; 'Get Free' – The Vines; 'How You Remind Me' – Nickelback; 'By The Way' – Red Hot Chili Peppers; 'Time for Heroes' – The Libertines; 'All My Life' – Foo Fighters.

Playlists: 'Where were you in '92?' – Kevin Robinson's playlist is on Spotify.

Favourite closing-time tracks: 'I Try' – Macy Gray; 'For the Dead' – Gene; 'Closing Time' – Semisonic; 'Walk Away' – Cast; 'Creep' – Radiohead; 'Under the Bridge' – Red Hot Chili Peppers; 'All the Small Things' – Blink182; 'Fade into You' – Mazzy Star; 'Glory Box' – Portishead; 'Bitter Sweet Symphony' and 'Lucky

Man' – The Verve; 'Sour Times' – Portishead; 'It Must Be Love' – Madness; Linger – The Cranberries; 'Waterloo Sunset' – The Kinks; 'Little Green Bag' – George Baker Selection.

EPILOGUE

In 2002, I moved to Auckland and have always enjoyed being in this country. My day jobs here have been more interesting and satisfying. I also love some of the smaller towns in New Zealand, particularly the Māniatoto region of Central Otago. Ranfurly is part of the Central Otago Rail Trail cycling route, with about seven hundred residents, and it's hard to beat for a quiet, relaxed town. I like my life here in NZ and although it's very different from my time in the Sugar Club, I always love to return home to the Boro' where my heart lies.

In 2004, there was a surprise half-page piece in *The Sun* newspaper by Dominic Mohan. He lauded The Pleasureheads as 'an early live music influence' and 'an exhilarating and inspiring experience... I think they split following a bizarre gardening accident.' At the end of the article, he said, '...live gigs are the best and, who knows, you may stumble upon the new Rolling Stones or even the new Pleasureheads.'

Recently, I was sent a Facebook message by a guy who went up to request a record from John Peel when he was DJ'ing at a nightclub. He got chatting and when Peel found out he was from Peterborough, he said, "Oh yeah, cool, I know The Pleasureheads from Peterborough." That made me feel very happy and I was excited to hear that my musical hero had remembered us and not just for the onion bhajis.

I loved my time in the group; we had three *NME* 'singles of the week' and released an album *Hard to Swallow*. Ultimately, we did okay, we had great fun and we lived to tell the tale. I feel I've always lived a rock-and-roll lifestyle, just minus the band for the last thirty years. Kev and Donny continue playing in bands to this day with the excellent Black Dog Murphy. There's even another band out there now who decided to use virtually the same name as us, just minus the 'The'. It's all about stewardship and somebody will always come along after you've finished. Our band still get together for a catch-up when we're back visiting the city on holiday. It's awesome to reconnect and I love them all.

After a while in Auckland, I did go to a couple of 'indie' clubs on Vulcan Lane with the possible idea of continuing DJ'ing. The local playlist, though, was totally different to the UK and very NZ-specific, think Crowded House, so I never returned to the DJ booth and hung up my headphones. I was ready for a rest anyway after working every weekend and public holiday for eleven years and you just can't recreate those special times. I do occasionally wake up in a cold sweat worried that my next track isn't cued up in time to play.

In 2019, I did something I always felt was very wrong and went against all my values – I gave up drinking. I was fed up with wasting too much time and feeling rough with a hangover, so I just gave up. While there were times when it felt odd – having spent all of my adult life having drinks – the benefits soon outweighed the negatives.

The same year, I promoted a new club venture in Auckland. I had missed promoting gigs and this was a perfect opportunity to start doing something worthwhile by opening a new social event. Clear Headed Social is an event for non-alcohol drinkers and provides a haven for people who like to go out and socialise but without the booze. I've partnered on the event with my pal, Zen, who is a fun, smart guy and a 'connector' of people. Almost everybody in Auckland city seems to know him, even though he's from Palmerston North. He has been running successful meet-up groups for years and we combined forces to create something different. So far, we've run a few events and the turnout has been really encouraging.

At one of those events, although she does drink alcohol sometimes, I met someone new. Jane is a very special person, who is smart, funny and attractive (yes, we have plenty in common). She is tall and olive-skinned, and we found it easy to talk to each other. We chatted for an hour at that first meeting and agreed to swap numbers. The next day, I texted her: 'Let's go out for a chat, I'm free on Tuesday or Thursday next week?' She said, 'Let's go out on Monday.' Maybe that indicates who's in charge, but that's fine. I don't mind. I said yes and we've been together ever since. Jane is fun, we gel together well and support each other and our goals.

I've just had my fifth anniversary sober and I'm feeling very content. I have a great relationship and I'm doing way better in every single way. I'm very lucky to have got a second chance of a great life. I'm now in a great relationship and we live together very happily with our two boys, Nate and Alfred. I'm happier now than I've ever been before.

It was a privilege to be a part of such an exciting Sugar Club night, which was able to be a part of so many people's social lives. Many music lovers started their own personal love affairs with our songs playing in the background, which is awesome. There's a lovely tribute on the Laughing Gravy Facebook page that says: 'Fantastic group, guys. I met my wife at the Shamrock Club in early 1990 (loved the Laughing Gravy). Thirty years later, still happily married, with three kids, still loving the music.'

EPILOGUE

Music is still a massive part of my life and I still love all the classics from the LG and Sugar Club, as well as new gems like Fontaines D.C. and Yard Act. I also still hate some pop stuff with a passion, like if I have the misfortune to hear Justin Timberlake's 'Can't Stop the Feeling!' at the shopping mall – particularly the bit that says, 'I got that sunshine in my pocket' and then I do feel quite sick. Worse still, I freeze dead on the school run when the tannoy system signals the end of the day at 3pm by playing 'Happy' by Pharrell Williams. As soon as he is let out of his class, I grab my lad by the hand, and we sprint past the other parents and kids to get out of the front gate and away from that awful sound.

Allen Adams, the city's punk music legend and part of the Sugar Club family, died unexpectedly in 2019 and there was an outpouring of sadness. Everyone fondly remembered his caring attitude, his uniqueness and his many musical projects. Steve was quoted in the local *Evening Telegraph*: 'We are all going to miss him. He was an old-school rocker. I hope Jesus hasn't lost his coat ticket, because he won't get his coat back until 3am.'

In 2021, Peterborough was again voted the 'worst place to live in the UK' – the third award in a row.

Steve is still hosting and attracting audiences with regular live music and Sugar Club nights at the Met Lounge on Bridge Street.

FINAL THOUGHTS

When this book is inevitably made into a blockbuster film, it will be co-directed by Ken Loach and Woody Allen, with a screenplay by Nick Hornby. I'd like stars from their prime to be portraying us. I'm really hoping for Paul Rudd (from *This is Forty*) to play me, Kev would be played by Brett from Suede, Steve by Peter Stringfellow, Martin by Noel Gallagher, Michelle and Kristy by Uma Thurman and Joni Mitchell. Andy S (who is alive and well in North Cambridgeshire) would be played by Kurt Cobain, Mary Leen Hagger by Meg Ryan (from *The Doors*) and Andy H would be played by Jack Black.

When I decided to write this memoir, I was reminded of the great comedian Eric Sykes who said of his autobiography, 'If I don't write it, then who will?'

LOVE AND THANKS FOR ALL THE INSPIRATION

Woodston Primary School, Mr Pearce, Orton Longueville School, Cyril Plant, Roy Marshall, Nick Hornby, Clive James, Tony Parsons, Dylan Jones, Peter Ackroyd, Salman Rushdie, George Orwell, David Baddiel, John Peel, Steve Lamacq, Jo Whiley, Paul Coyte, Chris Evans, Arthur Scargill, Dennis Skinner, Attila the Stockbroker, Jack Dee, Frank Skinner, Harry Hill, Reeves and Mortimer, Jo Brand, Sean Lock, Jerry Sadowitz, Morecambe and Wise, Harold Lloyd, Laurel and Hardy, Woody Allen, Walter Cornelius, Chris Turner, Peterborough Beer Festival, Broadgate FC, Gedney Hill FC, Peterborough Software, The Posh, Arsenal FC, Takapuna Tornado's FC and Greenhithe FC, Avondale Collaboration network, Paul Henry, I Love Avondale, MOTAT, NZ Football, Deaf Aotearoa.

Geordie, Bon, Stevie, Crossy, Mitch, Beebs and Gallo. The Sugar Club family, Met Lounge, the Sugar Club Survivors Facebook group, the Laughing Gravy Survivors Facebook group, Loaded club nights (Martin and Nathan), Steve Jason, Allen Adams, The Ostrich (aka Bogarts), The Still, Viva la Rock, Gaslight Comedy club.

The Pleasureheads and friends – Kev Murphy, Dean Nicholls, Pete Herron, Dave Colton, Joe Maccoll, Andy Donovan, Rob Jones, Mark Randall, John Conmy, Tony Judge, Andrew Clifton, Ann Johnson, Dominic Moran, James Cook.

Family – Mum, Dad, Jan and Mark, Rob and Caroline, Katie and Joe with Theo, Nathan and Sophie, Natasha and Glen with Albie, Matt and Zoe. Sharon and Peter. Julie and Kyle.

Jane, Nate, Alfred and Dennis the cat. Shane and Gill with Harrison and Lincoln, Zen Loo, Derek and Leigh.

'To Have and to Have Not' – Billy Bragg
'I Want You Back' – Hoodoo Gurus
'Wide Open Road' – The Triffids
'(Don't Go Back To) Rockville' – R.E.M.
'Beautiful Ones' – Suede
'I Am the Resurrection' – The Stone Roses

ABOUT THE AUTHOR

Pete Elderkin was born in Woodston, Peterborough and now lives in Auckland, NZ with Jane and their two boys, Nate and Alfred.

Contact Pete at www.sugargravypleasure.co.uk
or via Instagram – sugargravypleasure

This book is printed on paper from sustainable sources managed under the Forest Stewardship Council (FSC) scheme.

It has been printed in the UK to reduce transportation miles and their impact upon the environment.

For every new title that Troubador publishes, we plant a tree to offset CO_2, partnering with the More Trees scheme.

MORE TREES
LET'S PLANT A BILLION TREES

For more about how Troubador offsets its environmental impact, see www.troubador.co.uk/sustainability-and-community